Sailing with Jason and the Argonauts, Ulysses, the Vikings, and Other Explorers of the Ancient World

RANDOM HOUSE   NEW YORK

BEYOND THE EDGE OF THE SEA

Mauricio Obregón

All rights reserved under International and Pan-American Copyright
Conventions. Published in the United States by Random House, Inc.,
New York, and simultaneously in Canada by Random House
of Canada Limited, Toronto.

RANDOM HOUSE and colophon are registered trademarks
of Random House, Inc.

Library of Congress Cataloging-in-Publication Data

Obregón, Mauricio.
Beyond the edge of the sea: sailing with Jason and the Argonauts,
Ulysses, the Vikings, and other explorers of the ancient world /
Mauricio Obregón.
        p.   cm.
Includes bibliographical references.
ISBN 0-679-46326-7
1. Explorers.   2. Discoveries in geography.   3. Geography, ancient.
I. Title.
G88 .027   2001   930—dc21   00-027173

Random House website address: www.atrandom.com

Printed in the United States of America on acid-free paper

9 8 7 6 5 4 3 2

FIRST EDITION

Book design by Carole Lowenstein

Contents

Illustrations

Prologue

In order to see beyond the horizon, one must stand on someone else's shoulders, said Sir Isaac Newton.

The discovery of America was an extraordinary piece of luck, but luck brushes many a cheek with her wings, and only a few have the wit to grab her. Columbus did, but even he could not have crossed the ocean without "standing on the shoulders" of the ancient Greeks, who crossed the Black Sea and the Mediterranean; or of the Polynesians, who island-hopped across the apparently limitless South Seas; or of the Muslims, who rode and sailed the length of Asia to the Pacific; or of the Vikings, who crossed the North Atlantic to Newfoundland.

All seamen dream of home, but they pray for a fair wind, because they need to know what lies beyond the horizon. At sea there are no atheists, though atheists may often find themselves "at sea." On the high seas each prays to his own gods, for God has many faces.

Consequently, in order to understand the early navigators, one must not only know how they lived and where they sailed; one must also try to understand the winds that drove them, the stars that guided them, the women of whom they dreamed, and the gods they sometimes trusted, sometimes feared. We shall see how physically following the voyages sometimes confirms traditions and sometimes modifies them. And along the way, we will try to answer some age-old questions: How did the Argonauts get home? Where did Homer write his *Odyssey*? Are the "Indians" of South America descendants of the Polynesians?

Finally, my thanks go to all who, knowing that strangers are sent by Zeus, helped me on my way. They also know that I will never forget them.

BEYOND
THE EDGE
OF THE SEA

I

PEOPLES
AND GODS

Hɪsᴛᴏʀʏ ɪs ᴀ sʏᴍᴘʜᴏɴʏ of myths and legends. From the beginning, man's intelligence sketched the myths that would enable him to explain what he discovered, and from these myths collective memory built the legends that would make it possible to pass on the story.

When the Argonauts sailed east across the Black Sea to the Caucasus, and Odysseus west to the Pillars of Hercules, they broadened the limits of an earthbound sea already teeming with myths; and their adventures were handed down from generation to generation until Homer's poetry molded them at last into history. When the Polynesians sailed east across the Pacific to Easter Island and west across the Indian Ocean to Madagascar, their legends also went with them, but, unfortunately, they lacked a bard. Greeks and Polynesians, two antipodal peoples, explored more than half the world, yet they never met. They were very different, but their gods and their stars had much in common, for man seems to find similar solutions to similar problems wherever he may be.

The Greeks lived in walled cities, usually dominated by an acropolis, and their homes looked inward, not at the street but at an enclosed courtyard. The Polynesians, on the other hand, lived under wide thatched roofs, held up by open colonnades of palm wood. Their villages stood near the beach and generally included a house for meetings and for visitors, the *manaeba*. Though the Greeks watched jealously over their families and their property, the Polynesians usually owned at most a palm mat on which to sleep, with perhaps a small coffer at its head for a few belongings; all the rest was owned by the tribe. The Greeks buried their dead deep under great tumuli, such as can still be seen in Mycenae; the Polynesians buried them in small tombs right in front of their houses, and their children played on the tombs.

Each people sailed in character with the way each lived. The prudent Greeks usually sailed along coasts or toward the visible peaks of high islands, preferably in daytime and in summer. At night, or when the weather threatened, they pulled their ships up on the beach, singing to the rhythm of the waves, which helped raise the ship out of the water. (Caribbean fishermen still do this.) The Polynesians, on the contrary, were blue-water sailors, always ready to probe the deep.

Homer's world was a green ring of earth surrounding the known seas, the eastern Mediterranean and the Aegean. Around

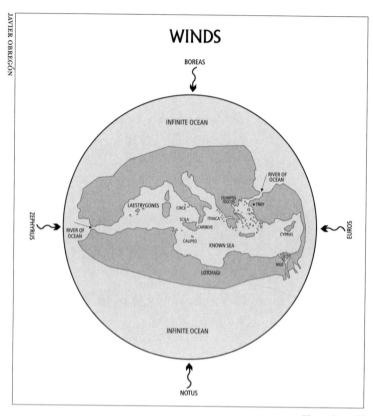

Homer's world

this world roared the Infinite Ocean, which fed the seas through two Rivers of Ocean, one from the east, where Helios, the Sun, rose from the Elysian Fields, and the other from the west, where he descended into Hades. The Polynesians' world, on the other hand, was the all-encompassing Ocean.

Mythology and its daughter, science, have always known whence life first came. To those who listen, the Gregorian chant of the waves speaks as clearly of gods as does the multitudinous rocking of the atoms, and it was out of the Infinite Ocean that the gods arose. In Babylon and in Egypt, Nun and Apsú floated above the all-encircling waters. In Hesiod's theogony and in Homer, Gaia, the Earth, and Uranus, the Sky, were born of Ocean, which was chaos, and engendered all the gods. For Polynesians it all began with Io, the waters; and the waters begot Rangui, the heavens, and Paapa, the earth. Even in Genesis, the Spirit of God moved first over the waters. And the Kogi Indians, Colombia's great mythologists, begin their story of creation with these words: "When all was dark, our mother was the Sea."

Having flown formation with an eagle down the god-infested canyon of Delphi, I myself need no further evidence for the ancient legends, and Homer's gods are easy to understand. But they are difficult to explain because the very word *God* obstructs the explanation in modern terms. The Greek gods are not otherworldly spirits but an integral part of society, an essentially feudal one in which everyone is subject to a superior being, or master of an inferior. There are servants, squires, chieftains, kings, tutelary spirits, nymphs, demigods, and gods; and within this framework one might do better to speak of "overlords" than of gods.

Since they form part of a tightly knit hierarchy, the Greek gods are always present to illuminate everyday things like bread and wine and death, with that transcendence necessary to sanity that we so lack today. When they want to be equivocal they use omens and signs, such as those that are interpreted through bird lore; but when they wish to be clearly understood they simply disguise themselves as men or women and speak. There is no question as to the gods' existence; the only question concerns their unpredictable behavior, for they are imperfect gods, and therefore quite real. One might say that whereas we have to make do with an imperfect faith in a perfect God, the Greeks were more comfortable with their perfect faith in imperfect gods. It is always difficult to seek perfection without first making one's peace with imperfection.

These imperfect gods act exactly as such, their always human reactions simply magnified by their wonderful powers, unlimited by the laws of nature but often limited by the desires and actions of another god. This has quite distinct advantages, not the least of which is that the gods, in order to avoid chaos, must enter into contracts or covenants not only with one another but also with men, thus laying the foundation for all subsequent justice by simple *do ut des* (tit for tat). This tradition lasts all the way to the covenants that underlie the Jewish, the Christian, and the Muslim faiths. In a world thus ordered, men also live according to a series of bilateral agreements with other men and simply pay the price whenever an agreement is broken, or, in the last resort, blame the gods. They can afford to live by a moral code (*mores* means "manners") rather than by what we would call ethics, and they can be virtuous and noble for reasons more sensible than the nagging avoidance of a sense of guilt. Revenge is to be feared more than guilt, and since an offense only breaks a bilateral contract, a third party such as the state can be quite lenient. We, on the other hand, always seem ready to unload our problems on the state and to throw morals out of the window, the young bent on replacing manners with fashion; the old, morals with money.

With the gods, a Greek minds his manners by offering the proper sacrifices at the proper times, which is pleasant because these ceremonies always include good food and drink for all. The word *sacrifice* does not imply denial; it simply means "to make sacred," and the ancients, while sacrificing, usually thought more of pleasure, while we think instinctively of pain. With his fellow men, a Greek minds his manners by willing observance of the laws of hospitality, which assume a joyously sacramental value because all strangers are wards of Zeus; by respecting his neighbor's property, his wife, and his slaves; and by giving the dead proper burial so that they may expediently cross the River.

Jason's and Odysseus' gods belonged to a third generation. Cronos, the Titan, had long since emasculated Uranus, his father, whose severed genitals had struck from the surf off Cyprus the spark that became Aphrodite, goddess of passion. In the next generation, Odysseus' patron, Athena, the goddess of intelligence, was born out of a Libyan lagoon while her father, Zeus, devoured her mother, Metis, the goddess of wisdom, so that Athena, like Aphrodite, would belong only to her father. In myth, as in everyday life, order and disorder must work together, Athena to bring light to men's eyes and Aphrodite to blind them.

Zeus loved not only goddesses but also women, and from these and from many other heaven-and-earth unions came a great court of demigods, nymphs, and sirens, among whom two great families stand out, those of the first heroes. Our very simplified family tree of the gods shows that those who adorn the earth and the sea with their adventures, like Odysseus, are descended from Hermes, the messenger, the voyager; and those whose caution

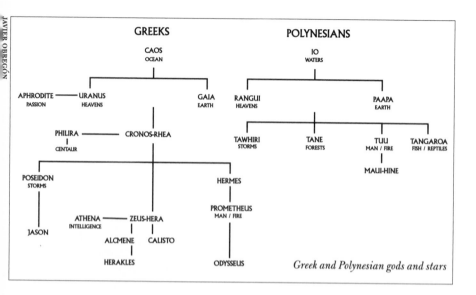

Greek and Polynesian gods and stars

leads them to treachery, like Jason, are descended from Poseidon, the treacherous sea.

Though the Polynesians left no epic poems, it is clear from their legends that their gods acted in much the same way as those of the Greeks. Rangui, the heavens, and Paapa, the earth, begot Tawhiri, god of storms; Tane, god of forests; Tangaroa, who stirred up the oceans and separated the fish (*ika*) from the reptiles (*tute*), and Tuu the warrior, forefather of man (Tiki) and woman (Hiné), whom he created out of red earth. His descendant, Mauí, would be the Polynesians' Odysseus. These second-generation gods of Polynesia were locked with their brothers and sisters in the dark embrace of their parents, and like the Titans of Greece, they decided to dethrone their progenitors. Together, they forced them apart, and ever since, at daybreak, the fragrance of Paapa's breast rises to heaven, and Rangui's lonely tears fall to earth as dew. Our diagram of Greek and Polynesian gods shows how strikingly similar they were. There were, of course, exceptions; gods enjoy exceptions.

A Polynesian legend tells us that the chief of one of the islands passed on after bequeathing his crown to whichever of his sons won a great *prau* race. When preparations were being made on the beach, his widow, Liktanur, came down with a long bundle under her arm and asked to be taken along. None of her sons agreed to be burdened with this "excess baggage" except the youngest, Jabro, whose chance of winning was nil. Off paddled the praus with Jabro bringing up the rear, until a breeze sprang up astern. Then Liktanur unpacked her bundle and brought out two long bamboo poles, some

Polynesian prau

coconut-fiber ropes, and a triangular palm mat, which she rigged as a sail. Then she taught Jabro how to sail with the wind and how to steer with his paddle. Amazed, and paddling like mad, the eldest brother, Timur, saw Jabro's prau sail ahead to win the race in three days. Ever since, Polynesians have used the claw sail.

Another legend tells us

that Mauí was stillborn because his father, Makea, forgot his prayers. Mauí was buried on the beach at the edge of the sea but was rescued and revived by the sorceress Hiné. When he grew up, he "went into" her, and he went out again only when he heard the song of a bird, and discovered death. Then he took a fire nail, which he had inherited from his ancestors (Mahu), and started such a conflagration that the god Tawhiri had to send enough rain to flood the world.

One day, Mauí got tired of being left behind when his older brothers went fishing and decided to hide under the floorboards of their prau. Once at sea, his brothers did not dare pitch him overboard, so they let him throw out a magic fishhook made out of a jawbone, which his godmother Muri-Ranga had given him, and it took Mauí only a few minutes to get a bite. But when he tried to pull in his catch, he could not move it, not even with the help of his brothers, who complained that the rising sun was in their eyes. Finally Mauí's catch came out of the water, and it was . . . an island! From then on Mauí was always invited along, and whenever he threw out his magic fishhook, he brought up another island, always with the rising sun in his eyes. When someone doubts this legend, Polynesians ask: "If Mauí did not fish up the islands, why are there seashells on their summits?"

Because the rising sun was always in their eyes, Mauí decided to tie it down, but he only succeeded in slowing its transit. The sun, in fact, lags behind the stars about a day every year, a good example of how the legends explained not only earthly phenomena, such as the Polynesian migration through the islands, but also astronomic facts useful for navigation (the Polynesian name for the sun ends in "-ra," like the name the ancient Egyptians gave it).

Another example is the story of the twins, Pipiri-Ma. Their parents tried to separate them and did not give them enough fish to eat, so the twins decided to escape. On the back of a star known as the Skybeatle, they flew from island to island until they came to Tahiti, the loftiest of all. From its summit, the twins leaped, but instead of falling they became fixed in the sky. Some say they are Shaula and Lesath, the last two stars in the tail of Scorpio; some say Gemini, the twin stars that the Polynesians call Hui-Tarar, *Hui* meaning "clusters."

The Greeks also recognized their gods in the constellations they observed. The giant Heracles (Hercules), after being left behind by the Argonauts and completing his labors, settled into the firmament as Orion, which resembles a giant with sword and shield. And the nymph Calisto, who was caught making love to Zeus and was condemned by the jealous Hera never again to bathe in Ocean's stream, became the constellation of the Great Bear, which, Calypso tells us in the *Odyssey,* is the only one that always circles above the horizon. We shall see that this navigational information gives us a clue as to where Homer composed his epic. Not only gods and goddesses but also women people the firmament: Andromeda, Cassiopeia, Berenice, and Hydra. And women, good or evil, are at the heart of the legends. Without Penelope, Circe, and Calypso there would have been no *Odyssey,* and without Medea no *Argonautica.*

II

WINDS AND
STARS

D ESPITE GODDESSES, nymphs, and sirens, the gods' favorite
weapons were not women but the elements. Zeus sent his
doves east and they returned from the west, so the ancient Greeks
knew that the earth was round, and Eratosthenes of Syene
(today's Aswan) calculated its circumference with remarkable ac-
curacy. He did this by measuring the shadow of a tower in
Alexandria on the summer solstice, when he knew that there
were no shadows in Syene because the sun was directly overhead, then equating angles with distances. Consequently, though
some ignorant sailors may later have forgotten it, the Greeks
knew they would not fall off the edge of the world.

In the second century B.C., Hipparchus of Rhodes established
that the different parts of the globe inclined more or less toward

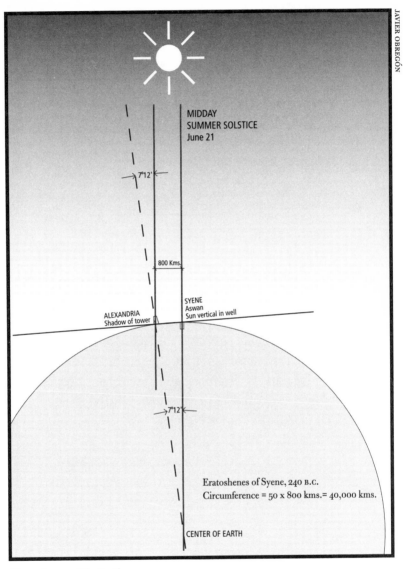

MIDDAY
SUMMER SOLSTICE
June 21

7°12'

800 Kms.

ALEXANDRIA
Shadow of tower

SYENE
Aswan
Sun vertical in well

7°12'

Eratoshenes of Syene, 240 B.C.
Circumference = 50 x 800 kms.= 40,000 kms.

CENTER OF EARTH

Circumference of the Earth

the sun not only because of the seasons but also depending on latitude, and he divided the globe into five climates, or inclinations. In the middle were the tropics (the Greek word means the keel of the globe); north and south of the tropics were the two temperate zones, where men lived; and beyond them were the polar zones. Still today the tropics of Cancer and Capricorn limit the zone on which the sun's rays fall vertically, and the temperate zones end in the Arctic and Antarctic Circles, beyond which the sun never altogether rises in winter or altogether sets in summer.

Climates and trade winds

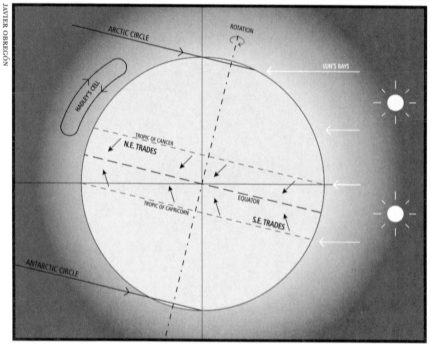

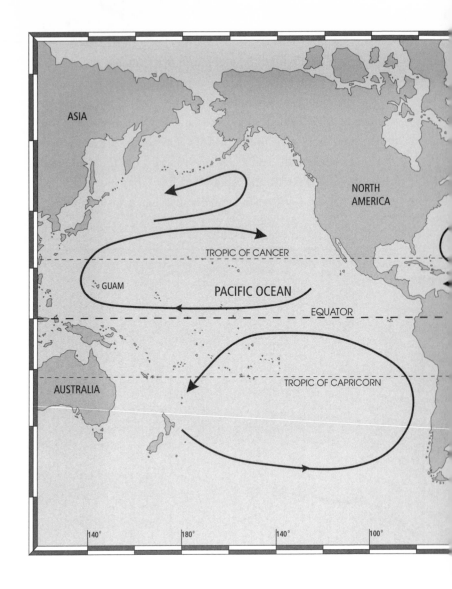

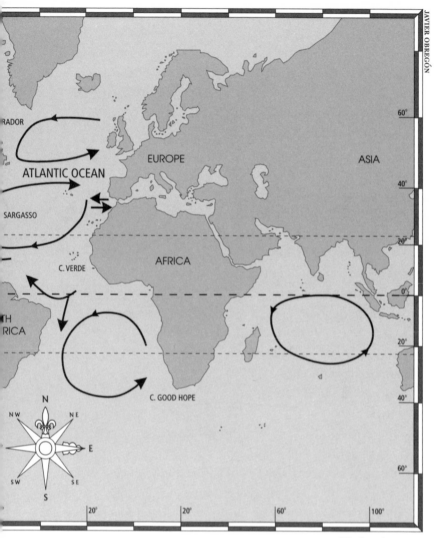

RADOR

ATLANTIC OCEAN

SARGASSO

C. VERDE

EUROPE

ASIA

AFRICA

H
RICA

C. GOOD HOPE

60°

40°

20°

0°

20°

40°

60°

N
NW   NE
W   E
SW   SE
S

20°   20°   60°   100°

Winds and currents

JAVIER OBREGÓN

In the tropics, the sun produces huge "balloons" of hot air that rise and make room below for cold polar air, but since the earth's surface revolves fastest at the equator (close to the speed of sound), the resulting winds do not blow out of the north and

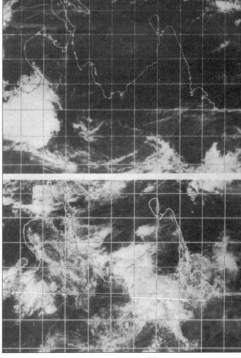

south but out of the northeast and southeast. Obeying Coriolis' theorem, they end up circling clockwise in the northern oceans and counterclockwise in the southern, creating trade winds in the west and monsoons in the east. Where the northeast and southeast trades meet in the tropics, clouds congregate along the "convergence zone," which follows the sun's seasonal migrations north and south and, as it passes, produces regular rainy seasons.

Everywhere, warm air cools as it rises, and its vapors condense, giving birth to clouds: cotton-wool cumuli up to some fifteen thousand feet, sheets of stratus up to twenty, and feathery cirrus up to thirty. If the updraft is strong enough, Zeus' anvil begins to thunder, and the infernal cumulonimbus boils

Monsoons

with the god's lightning up to some sixty thousand feet. I flew into one once in an old and overloaded DC-3, and with elevators, wheels, and flaps down, I still shot up at more than three thousand feet per minute until the god grew tired of me and threw me

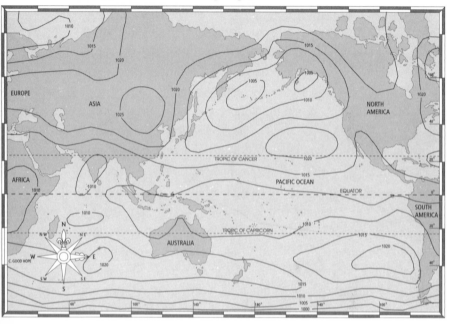

Monsoons (weather map)

out like a toy. But the gods always call their family back to order, and the morning sea breeze returns to the waves in the evenings as if to sleep with the Nereids, the daughters of Ocean. In the end, every family of beings adapts to its own conditions, and each sea and each sky knows its denizens. Navigators learn to recognize them: pelicans, for example, never fly much more than twenty-five nautical miles from shore, and sharks and dolphins stay close to shore in temperate waters, while in the tropics they roam the high seas.

The Greeks and Polynesians identified directions with winds whose personality, smell, and taste they easily recognized. For the Greeks, out of the north sprang Boreas, like a dry white wine; and for the Polynesians Tokelau, the name of the northernmost Polynesian islands. Out of the east, steady Euros blew for the Greeks; and for the Polynesians Marangay, which means "constant as a woman" (whether because of fidelity or insistence we do not know). Out of the south, Notus raged with fiery passion; as did Tonga, named for the Polynesians' southernmost islands and their fierce inhabitants. And out of the west stormed temperamental Zephyrus, with its promise of rain; and Parapu, which blew out of the land of Polynesian Spirits. Still today out of the north mistrals, meltemis, Santa Anas, and harmattans worry Frenchmen, Greeks, Californians, and Nigerians; Catalans tend to commit suicide when the tramontana blows out of the north. (Valleys sometimes channel the great winds—for instance, the powerful mistrals pour down the valley of the Rhône onto the Mediterranean, where they are called tramontanas.) And out of the south siroccos, khamsins, Notus, and foehns craze Italians, Levantines, Yugoslavs, and even the Swiss, who prefer to commit their rare crimes of passion when foehn blows hot.

Currents are also produced by the rotation of the earth, by the great winds, and by fast-flowing, deep-sea rivers. As with air masses, cold waters displace warm. In addition, salt waters displace fresh waters, and the Greek Rivers of Ocean still exist: out of the Atlantic and the Black Sea, surface currents run through

WINDS

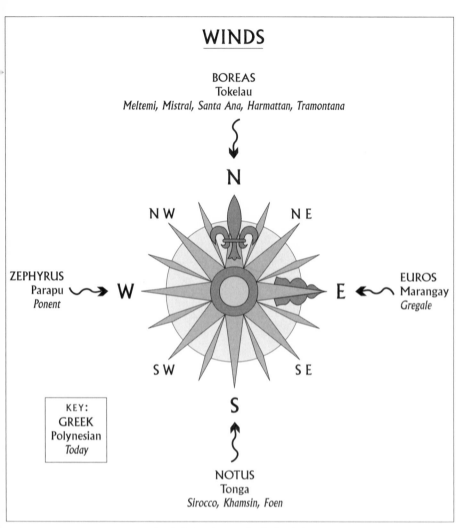

BOREAS
Tokelau
Meltemi, Mistral, Santa Ana, Harmattan, Tramontana

N

N W   N E

ZEPHYRUS
Parapu
Ponent
W

E
EUROS
Marangay
Gregale

S W   S E

S

KEY:
GREEK
Polynesian
Today

NOTUS
Tonga
Sirocco, Khamsin, Foen

Greek, Polynesian, and today's winds

the Strait of Gibraltar and the Hellespont to replace the water that the sunny Mediterranean loses by evaporation, while the Mediterranean slips its saltier brine underneath. Consequently, in the straits the surface current flows into the Mediterranean while on the bottom the current flows out. During World War II, German and Italian submarines used both currents to float silently in and out of the straits with their engines turned off, so that the British, in Gibraltar, could not detect their throbbing. The sea is also attracted by the Sun and the Moon, creating tides; when the two are in line with the wind and the coast acts as a funnel, water piles up, as in the Canadian Bay of Fundy, where tide levels vary by as much as fifteen meters. It may seem strange, but what has changed most with the centuries is the firmament. Though the stars hardly move within their own constellations, we have seen that, perhaps thanks to Maui, each year all of them together gain a day relative to the sun. Thus, even though our calendar was designed to correct this, the sun's position among the stars on any given date today is different from what it was for the Assyrians and for the Egyptians, a fact that confuses some astrologers. What is more, as Hipparchus pointed out in the second century B.C., the earth, as it spins on its way around the sun, wobbles sleepily like a top, its poles completing every twenty-six thousand years a circle of precession in space whose diameter is about a third of that of the globe. Consequently, when referring to Homer's stars, one must figure that the projection of the North Pole then lay between Kochab, on top of the bowl of the Little Dipper, and Giansar, in Draco's tail; and all the other stars apparently circled around that point just as surely as they circle

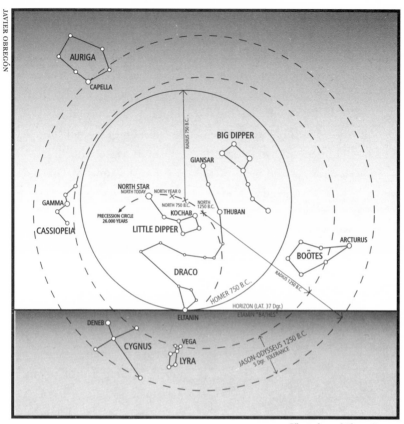

The pole and "home" stars

around our North Star today. In the days of Jason and Odysseus, and of the first Polynesian navigators, the pole lay even farther back in the heavens, near Thuban, in Draco.

How far the stars swing down as they circle around the celestial projection of the North Pole depends on the latitude of the observer. Seen from the equator, all the constellations rise in the east and set in the west; seen from the North Pole, the constellations simply circle overhead, and none of them ever sets. Consequently, the farther north the observer stands in the Northern Hemisphere, the greater is the number of constellations that stay permanently above the horizon. We have noted that in the *Odyssey*, Calypso says that the Big Dipper is "the only constellation which never bathes in Ocean's stream." Our diagram shows that if Homer had lived north of thirty-seven degrees north latitude, Eltanin, at the head of the great constellation of Draco, would, from his point of view, also have stayed dry above the horizon. In order for the Dipper to be the *only* constellation that never set, Homer must have been familiar with only latitudes south of thirty-seven degrees north; and his language places him near Asia Minor and not much farther south than Cyprus.

Consequently, Homer's stars seemed to me to indicate that he must have lived on Cyprus, so I flew to Cyprus to try my proposal on Vasso Karageorgis, director of the Cyprus Archaeological Museum, in Nicosia. Far from laughing, he took me down to the museum's basement and showed me a collection of implements and

Penelope's chair

furniture that were in use in Cyprus in the eighth century B.C., when Homer lived, and I immediately saw that they were strikingly similar to those that modern archaeology has shown were in use in the rest of Greece in the thirteenth century B.C., when Jason and Odysseus sailed. So a Cypriot, Homer, could have known from experience how his heroes lived five hundred years before his time, and could have described, as he did, their arms, their clothes, their implements, and their furniture. Cyprus was always the most conservative outpost of ancient Greece, and in Homer's day, though the rest of Greece had already adopted the Phoenician alphabet, the Cypriots still used pictographs similar to those used in Jason's and Odysseus' time, to engrave on clay tablets extensive lists of ships, oarsmen, and supplies much like Homer's "catalogue of ships." Moreover, Cyprus did not play an active role against Troy, which might explain why Homer is so impartial between the Greeks and the Trojans.

My hypothesis answers four ancient questions: 1) Why was Homer so sure that the Big Dipper was the only constellation that never dipped below the horizon? 2) How, in the eighth century B.C., could he describe so well the implements used five centuries earlier? 3) Where could he have obtained his detailed and apparently complete "catalogue of ships"? And 4) Why was he, a Greek, so neutral in his treatment of the Trojan war?

Homer several times mentions the zenith of his heroes' stars, so it must have been traditional that Jason and Odysseus knew which stars faithfully "overheaded" their home ports, at least within the few degrees of error that one may make when measuring the vertical without instruments. Only one generation sepa-

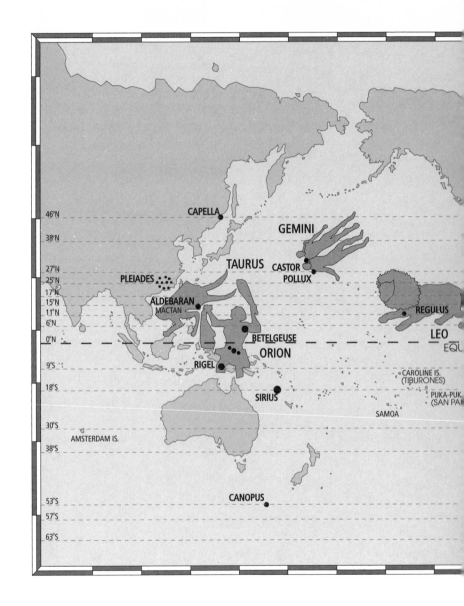

CAPELLA

GEMINI

TAURUS   CASTOR
PLEIADES   POLLUX

ALDEBARAN
MACTAN   REGULUS

BETELGEUSE   LEO
RIGEL   ORION   EQ

CAROLINE IS.
(TIBURONES)

PUKA-PUK
(SAN PA
SIRIUS
SAMOA

AMSTERDAM IS.

CANOPUS

46°N
38°N
27°N
25°N
17°N
15°N
11°N
6°N
0°N
9°S
18°S
30°S
38°S
53°S
57°S
63°S

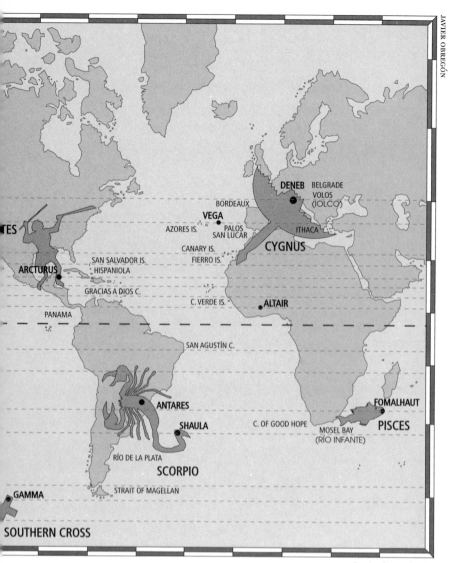

ES

DENEB BELGRADE
VOLOS
(IOLCO)

BORDEAUX

VEGA

AZORES IS. PALOS
SAN LÚCAR ITHACA

CANARY IS.
SAN SALVADOR IS. FIERRO IS. CYGNUS
ARCTURUS HISPANIOLA

GRACIAS A DIOS C.

PANAMA C. VERDE IS. ALTAIR

SAN AGUSTÍN C.

FOMALHAUT

ANTARES

SHAULA C. OF GOOD HOPE PISCES
MOSEL BAY
(RÍO INFANTE)

RÍO DE LA PLATA

SCORPIO

GAMMA STRAIT OF MAGELLAN

SOUTHERN CROSS

Latitude navigation

rated the two seafarers, and only one degree of latitude separated their home ports; hence, when they were home they must both have noted that Arcturus in the constellation of Boötes, Vega in Lyra, Capella in Auriga, Deneb in Cygnus, and Mirfak in Perseus passed overhead. Each of these is clearly recognizable with the naked eye. Consequently, though Homeric navigators could never tell how far east or west they had gone, they could quite easily judge whether they were north or south of their home latitude, the latitude traveled by their home stars. Then they could sail north or south to get under that latitude and sail home east or west toward the home stars' rising or setting. To sail north or south was no problem, for during the day Boreas in the north and Notus in the south were easy winds to recognize, and at night, if the Bear flew below the horizon, Cassiopeia flew high, and vice versa, and both of them serve to find north.

Homer says: "There are times when the great sea is darkened by a soundless swell. It knows that a gale is on its way; but that is all it knows, and the waves cannot begin their march . . . 'til the wind sets in steadily from one side or the other." Who but a sailor could speak thus? So it seems probable that at some stage of his life Homer may have been a sailor. Tradition says that Homer may have been blind. Why should we not hypothesize that he was a Cypriot who had been a sailor and knew his stars? Perhaps the gods blinded him, as they did Phineus, whom we shall meet later, because he knew too much. . . .

III

SHIPS AND NAVIGATION

Sketchy and few are the contemporary illustrations of Homeric ships that have come down to us, but it is interesting that the earliest was found in Iolcos, Jason's home, where it is still to be seen in the Athanassakeion Archaeological Museum of modern Vólos. Our best information comes from a careful sailor's reading of the Homeric texts, beginning with information about Ulysses' own ship and with the description of the boat that Calypso helped him build. With one oarsman on each side and a walkway in between, the lean warships that went to Troy cannot have been much wider than three meters at their beamiest point. They carried fifty men, one to each oar, so they must have been some twenty-five meters long on the waterline (to which the prow and the flying stern would have to be added). Homer tells us that

JAVIER OBREGÓN

when Odysseus was wrecked off Sicily, the fir mast fell aft and crushed the helmsman's skull, so it must have been some twelve meters high.

As for the sail, Homer says that when a favorable wind blew, the mast was stepped and steadied with stays that were called *tonos,* and every sailor knows that, in a big wind, each stay sings its own "tone." Then the yard and square sail were hoisted. When the wind died, the sail was brailed up to the yard, the yard lowered, and the mast unstepped and stowed, so the rig was clear.

The hull was painted black with pitch, and Homer refers to two beams some two meters long that transfixed it fore and aft of the oarsmen. These beams were called *threnoi* (they groaned like a threnody), and their exposed ends served as stirrups for sailors coming aboard. When the wind was steady, I think they were also used to make fast the sheets, or *pous,* that held the tacks of the sail, but when the wind was treacherous, the pous surely passed around the threnus to gain friction, and were held in the helmsman's grip. The boards of early Greek hulls were "sewn" together, but later they were "stapled" together with bronze harmonia, and the twenty-five benches, joined along their middle by a wooden gangway, served also as crossbeams or thwarts, and on each gunwale, leather thongs secured the oars to their *kleis* (keys or tholepins). The height of the stern is also clear, since Achilles rested his hand on it while standing on the beach. Given its length, we can calculate that the ship's draft, fully loaded, must have been about a meter.

The gunwales were not much more than half a meter above water. So how did the Greeks keep the waves from splashing into their ship? In southern Turkey, I rounded Cape Gelidonya, approached the steep cliff at Kaş, hove to, and hailed the modern cliff-hangers in their lofty camp. George Bass and his team from Texas A&M's Institute of Nautical Archaeology were comparing the remains of the ships they had found, and both here and at Cape Gelidonya were the remains of the wicker rail that Homer describes and calls *pararumata*. It is like the one still used by Arab *lamu* dhows to keep the crest of waves from breaking over the bulwark.

Ancient Greek ships could not sail close to the wind. When it blew adverse but light, they lowered the yard and mast and rowed; and when it freshened, they either beached or hove overboard the perforated anchor stone. I spotted one on the sea bottom and, diving closer, found it was still being used by a fisherman. Greeks use their antiquities, but they "protect" them from foreigners, as we found out when we had sailed late out of Piraeus and decided to drop anchor for the night, snug between the high Diasporidae rocks. In the moonlight, we went over the side with our snorkels and, finding the bottom strewn with broken amphorae, recovered the best pieces. But once we climbed on board, the owner, a prudent Scot, made us throw them back. We revisited the Diasporidae on our way back, and what did we find? An enormous dredge excavating the sand, amphorae and all.

How fast were these ships? According to Apollonius of Rhodes, it took the Argonauts twelve hours to row thirty miles to Samothrace from Lemnos and from there to the Hellespont, so they made two and a half knots rowing. From Cape Acherusias (Ereğli) to Cape Carambis (Kerempe Cape) and again from Sinop to the Amazons' river Thermodon, *Argo* made five knots, one hundred and twenty miles in twenty-four hours, a good average speed under sail with a following wind. According to Homer, Odysseus' son Telemachus sailed one hundred miles from Pylos to Ithaca in twelve hours before a godsent wind, and Nestor made the same time over the same distance from Lesbos to Geraistos (today's Carystus) in southern Euboea. So they made eight knots, a pretty godsent speed, but not out of line with the modern formula for maximum hull speed, 1.6 times the square root of the waterline in feet.

The Polynesians' problem was not to follow a coast but to sail the high seas in search of one more island. They used ships that they called *praus,* quite similar to those of the ancient Greeks but often provided with outriggers and double hulls. Pliny the Elder said that the ships of Ceylon had bows at each end, and Albo, Magellan's navigator, said that in Guam they had sterns out of their prows. Captain Cook reported that they sometimes carried up to one hundred men. Like Greek ships, they used stone anchors, and their hulls were built on ribs with boards sewn together end to end with cord made out of coconut fiber, and caulked with breadfruit sap heated with burning sennit.

Polynesians

The Polynesians had the claw sails we met in Timur and Jabro's legend, which could get much closer to the wind than Greek square sails, and they sailed up to one hundred miles a day.

The Greeks and the Polynesians both had maps, but none of

them has come down to us. In the second century A.D. Ptolemy, an Alexandrian Greek, wrote the famous *Geography,* which became the basis for almost all maps until the High Renaissance, but even he left no maps, only detailed descriptions and data on latitude and longitude.

In 1778 when Captain Cook discovered Hawaii, he wrote: "How shall we account for this [Polynesian] Nation spreading itself over such a vast ocean?" We know that as the Polynesians approached an island, they watched clouds massing over the land and crisscross wave patterns. They also knew that long-tailed cuckoos, for example, migrated in September from Tahiti to New Zealand, and golden plovers from Tahiti to Hawaii, while seabirds seldom strayed more than eighteen miles

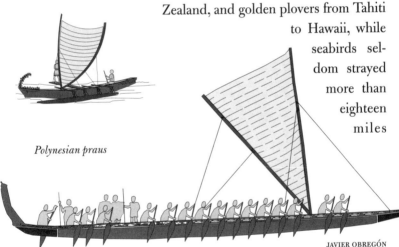

Polynesian praus

JAVIER OBREGÓN

from their nests. And they carried dogs, aptly called *moi-moi,* which barked when they smelled land. All this they called *etak.* Like the ancient Greeks, they used latitude navigation, following known stars down their east-west paths, a method they called *fanakenga;* they also knew which stars "overheaded" each group of islands. Canopus (Atutaki) passed over New Zealand; Rigel over the Solomons; Beta Arietis over Hawaii; and Sirius (Moan-Faiti) over Fiji.

Off these paths, the old Polynesians with whom I have talked claim they use a star compass (*kaweinga*) based on the assumption that stars rise and set always at the same bearing from the observer. For instance, they say that Tau Mailap (Altair) stands just north of east when it rises and just north of west when it sets; Tarara (Shaula, one of the twins in the tail of Scorpio) rises in the southeast and sets in the southwest; Vega rises in the northeast and sets in the northwest; and Antares rises in the southeast and sets in the southwest. This system has been tried in temperate zones and found wanting, because as one varies one's latitude, the bearing (or azimuth) of rising or setting stars also varies.

One night in the Caribbean I set out to sea from Cartagena in order to catch the wind into the San Blas islands, on the Panamanian side of the Colombian border. It was the season when the trades had not yet hit their stride, but on this night they and their waves attacked us with a vengeance. Our sail was torn, our propeller shaft came loose and jammed our rudder, and our compass was smashed. It took us some time to pull ourselves together, but once the propeller shaft was removed and our sail stitched together, we decided to sail on, guided only by the Polynesian star compass. After one of the most beautiful nights I have spent at sea (in silence, of course, with no engine), dawn saw us sail through the reef toward Isla de Pinos, to the welcome of the smiling Cuna Indians.

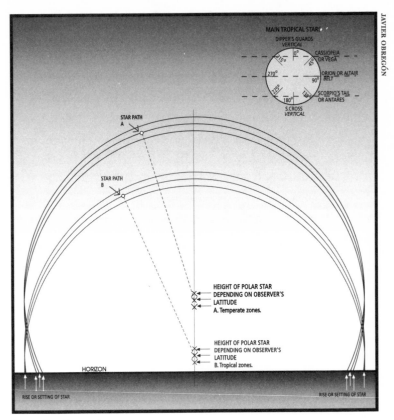

Polynesian star compass

Why does the star compass work only in the tropics? The formula is:

$$\text{cosine of azimuth of star} = \frac{\text{sine of declination of star}}{\text{cosine of latitude of observer}}$$

but for those who abhor trigonometrical formulas, I have worked out a graphic demonstration. In "A" we go from one latitude to another with the polestar standing high—in other words in a temperate zone; in "B" we make the same variations of latitude with the polestar lying close to the horizon, as in the tropics. In the first case, as we move from one latitude to another, the star we are watching rises and sets in very different places; in the second, it is not affected. So in the tropics, the latitude of the observer does not affect the Polynesians' star compass.

One question remains to be addressed. With these ships and with these methods of navigation, could the Polynesians have reached South America? Most South American Indians have Oriental features, as opposed to the aquiline looks of North and Central Americans, who apparently came across the Bering Strait and migrated south. The Polynesians' migrations generally ran eastward, for example from Samoa to the Marquesas, and all their staple foods were of Asian origin except the sweet potato (coconuts floated unaided from Asia to South America). Their Lapita pottery has been excavated in increasingly more recent civilizations, traveling all the way east to Easter Island (Rapa Nui), and there the remaining natives speak an East Polynesian dialect. All of this indicates migration toward South America. The voyage from Easter Island to South America is no longer than the one we know the Polynesians made from the Marquesas to Hawaii and to Easter Island itself. The Polynesians knew how to survive for weeks on birds potted in their own fat, live water hens, sweet potatoes, and coconut milk, with fermented palm toddy (*tuba*) to keep them happy. So why should they not have made the final jump to South America?

We have seen that Polynesian legends tell a beautiful story of

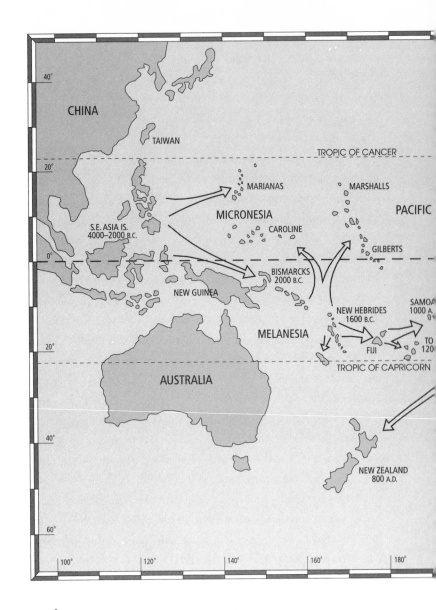

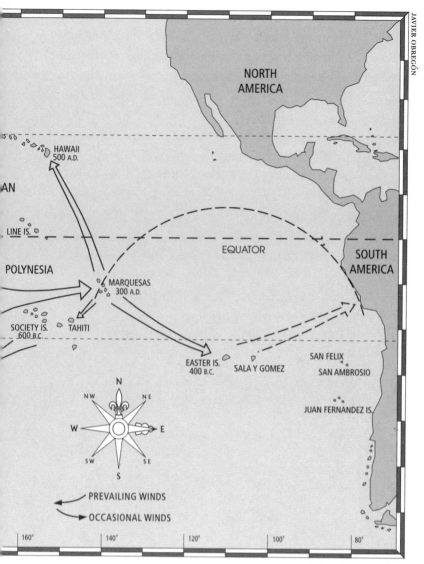

JAVIER OBREGÓN

NORTH
AMERICA

HAWAII
500 A.D.

AN

LINE IS.

EQUATOR

SOUTH
AMERICA

POLYNESIA

MARQUESAS
300 A.D.

SOCIETY IS.   TAHITI
600 B.C.

EASTER IS.   SALA Y GOMEZ
400 B.C.

SAN FELIX
SAN AMBROSIO

JUAN FERNANDEZ IS.

N
NW   NE

W   E

SW   SE
S

PREVAILING WINDS

OCCASIONAL WINDS

160°   140°   120°   100°   80°

Polynesian migrations

how the claw sail could have brought Mauí, island after island, across the Pacific, with the rising sun in his eyes—in other words in the general direction of America. But we have also seen that the trade winds in the South Pacific blow stubbornly out of the east, and Thor Heyerdahl, in his raft *Kon-Tiki,* showed that the Indians could have used them to migrate westward, toward Asia rather than toward America. How could the Polynesians have migrated against the prevailing winds?

I propose a sailor's answer, so far unchallenged: if, like Columbus, one is going to sail across an ocean toward a great continent, one goes with the prevailing wind, as Columbus did; but if, like the Polynesians, one is going to sail out into an apparently limitless ocean in search of an island that may or may not be there, it is wiser to wait for one of those days when the wind blows contrary to its prevailing direction. Then, if the island does not turn up, instead of being blown away indefinitely, one can simply wait for the prevailing wind to return, and can sail home to try again another day. So it makes good nautical sense that the Polynesians should have made use of occasional rather than prevailing winds, migrating eastward when exceptional winds blew, and not westward with the trades.

Columbus' journal of October 13, 1492, says that American Indians had canoes carved out of single tree trunks, some big enough for forty-five men, but his journal of October 26, 1492, and Michele de Cuneo's account of October 15, 1495, both affirm that the Indians had no sails. This is not surprising, because paddles raised in a stiff trade wind can easily propel a canoe. At the end of his fourth voyage, Columbus was marooned for a year at

St. Ann's Bay in Jamaica (where I searched unsuccessfully for his last two caravels, and where the Institute of Nautical Archaeology has carried on). Méndez and Fieschi had to rig a square sail on an Indian canoe, which they had acquired in exchange for a chamber pot. They then sailed and paddled with a dozen Indians all the way to Santo Domingo to get help, and as far as I know, the first to mention an Indian sail was Balboa, some twenty years after the discovery of America.

So what happened to the claw sails the Polynesians must have bequeathed the Indians if, in fact, they sailed to South America? The answer probably lies in the fact that on the Pacific coast of South America one sometimes sees sails similar to claw sails, while in the Caribbean, Spanish square sails are still the norm. It

DE BRY

Indians with paddles

seems clear that if the Polynesians' sails reached the Pacific coast of America, they did not make it across the continent. On the other hand, Columbus tells us that Indians of the Caribbean always used paddles, which are typical of the Pacific, whereas oars are typical of the Mediterranean and the Atlantic. So paddles, which are more useful in continental rivers than sails, seem to have made it from the Pacific to the Caribbean, whereas sails did not.

Both the Greeks and the Polynesians knew how to use the stars, which came from the family tree of their gods, but the Greeks preferred coastal navigation and island-hopping, and if forced to face the open sea used latitude navigation alone, whereas the Polynesians were blue-water sailors, capable of criss-crossing oceans not only by latitude navigation but also with their own star compass.

Unfortunately, of the migrations of the Polynesians we have no complete accounts, though we do know roughly how and when they reached each group of islands. But of the voyages of Jason and Odysseus we have good accounts, principally Pindar's Fifth Ode, Apollonius' *Argonautica,* and Homer's *Odyssey;* and, to check geography, we have the journey that Scylax prepared for Darius the Great, the king of Persia, at the beginning of the sixth century B.C. With these and other documents in hand, let us follow from the air and by sea the voyages of the Argonauts and of Odysseus, to see how the ancient Greeks widened their world from the Aegean, east to the Caucasus and west to the Pillars of Hercules.

IV

EASTWARD:
THE ARGONAUTICA

HOW DID THE GREEKS DISCOVER that eastward the world did not end in the Black Sea?

Pindar tells us that King Pelias of Iolcos, a descendant of Poseidon, god of the treacherous sea, usurped the throne of his half brother Aeson, Jason's father, and that an oracle warned him that his challenger would arrive wearing only one sandal. Aeson sent young Jason to the top of Mount Pelion to be brought up by Cheiron, the wise centaur who was the tutor of heroes (perhaps, as Machiavelli points out, because a great leader needs animal instincts as well as human virtues). As soon as he grew up, Jason decided to go down to Iolcos, (today's Vólos) to claim his throne in public, and as he crossed the river carrying an old crone who begged for his help one of his sandals remained stuck in the mud.

When Jason put her down, the crone turned out to be Hera, the goddess of survival, who would be his patron.

Wily old Pelias, forewarned by the sandal, offered to give up the throne if Jason would prove himself by sailing "to the end of the world" to recover the Golden Fleece of the ram on whose back Aeson's other children, Phrixus and Helle, had escaped their stepmother's wrath. Helle fell from the ram's back between Europe and Asia, christening the Hellespont, but Phrixus flew on to Colchis, at the world's end, where he left the fleece on top of a great oak. Pelias said he was haunted by the threat of a seven-year famine for Iolcos if the Golden Fleece was not brought home. Poor Jason, having "gone public," could not refuse this challenge.

Jason was a handsome northern aristocrat with long blond hair who carried two spears, one for throwing and one for thrusting, and covered his woolen underwear (typical of his country, Magnesia) with a leopard skin. Pindar tells us that he was *amekanos,* not very resourceful. But Jason did have one redeeming virtue, and a very aristocratic one: he knew how to pick the men who possessed the skills he lacked. That is why *The Argonautica* is named not for Jason but for a shipload of heroes.

First Jason recruited Argus, the engineer, to build the ship that would bear his name, and balanced him with the musical wizard who could best handle what an engineer does not understand: Orpheus, son of Apollo and the Muse Calliope. Next came Tiphys, the great helmsman, supported by Zetes and Calais, the winged sons of Boreas, the north wind. Then Mopsus and Idmon, two seers, and two boxers, Pollux and Castor, who were twins. Lynceus, the lynx-eyed, came with his mad brother Idas, who saw reality beyond appearances and fearlessly sang out the truth. Amidships rowed Ancaeus, the giant who knew the stars, and Heracles, the heavy club-carrying superhero, cloaked in his lion skin and waited upon by his beauteous young page, Hylas. Finally, Peleus, the adventurer, completed the list of fifty men.

Jason delayed all he could, and the crew even offered his command to Heracles, who refused. But faced with the protest of *Argo*'s talking keel (Athena's gift) Jason ran his ship down the beach on rollers, and finally put to sea.

The weeping of the women of Iolcos receded as Orpheus' lyre set the rhythm of the oars, and *Argo* glided through the morning mists across the sleeping gulf of Pegasae and out into the sea. Across the centuries an echo of Orpheus' song has come down to us: a cuneiform musical score engraved on a clay tablet dating from about the time of the Argonauts was found not long ago in Ugarit, Syria. Interpreted on a reconstructed lyre, it sounds as if it could well have paced fifty long-distance oarsmen. *The Argonautica* was under way.

Apollonius tells us that Notus, the south wind, made up at last, and the tired Argonauts stepped the mast and hoisted the sail. So we know that they rounded dark Cape Sepias to the east and, leaving the island of Skiathos to starboard, ran north with wind and current up the magnificent coast of Magnesia. The "tone" of the stays took over Orpheus' song, and fish played in the roiling wake as the Argonauts passed under Mount Pelion, whose seaward slopes dress for summer with herbs, flowers, fruit, walnuts, pines, and olives. Cheiron the centaur saw them come and galloped down to the beach. His wife, Chariclo, fol-

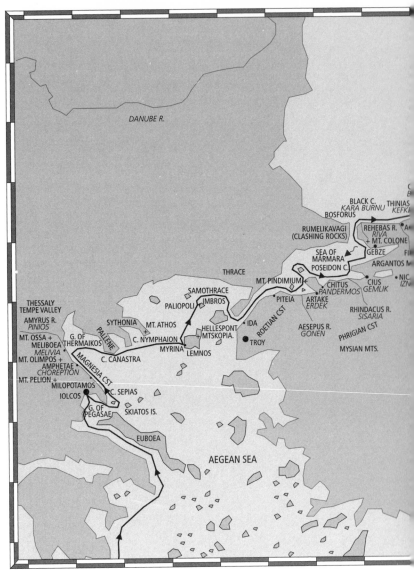

The Argonautica, *outbound*

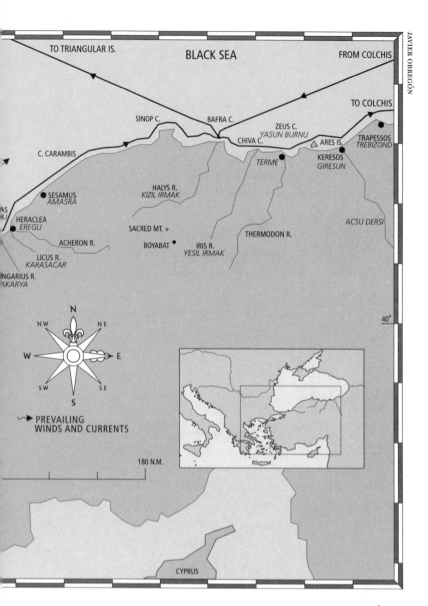

JAVIER OBREGÓN

TO TRIANGULAR IS.

BLACK SEA

FROM COLCHIS

TO COLCHIS

SINOP C.   BAFRA C.

ZEUS C.
YASUN BURNU

CHIVA C.

TRAPESSOS
TREBIZOND

ARES IS.

C. CARAMBIS

TERME

KERESOS
GIRESUN

SESAMUS
AMASRA

HALYS R.
KIZIL IRMAK

ACSU DERSI

HERACLEA
EREGLI

SACRED MT. +

THERMODON R.

ACHERON R.

BOYABAT

IRIS R.
YESIL IRMAK

LICUS R.
KARASACAR

NGARIUS R.
AKARYA

40°

N
NW   NE
W   E
SW   SE
S

PREVAILING
WINDS AND CURRENTS

180 N.M.

CYPRUS

lowed, carrying the infant Achilles so that he might watch his father, Peleus, sail by, and begin to dream of Troy. All this surely happened at beautiful Milopotamos under high Tsangarada.

When Dolop's tomb came into sight, the wind left *Argo*'s sail and the Argonauts decided to beach her at Amphetae, which means "farewell," happy to spend two days offering sacrifices—in other words feasting—before finally leaving their homeland. The tomb could be any of the high rocks that rise out of this theatrical seacoast, and Amphetae was probably the beach at Choreftion, which means "the place for ceremonies or choirs," under steep and shady Zagora.

On the third day Notus returned, and the Argonauts sailed past Meliboea (today's Melivia), then under two-thousand-meter Mount Ossa, up the scarred flanks on which the Titans of old had tried to pile Mount Pelion in order to challenge the Olympians. They passed the mouth of the river Amirus (today's Piniós), which still plows a broad furrow through dusty Thessaly to create the verdant valley of Tempe, "filled with the song of the nightingale," says Apollonius. In the evening they were abeam snowcapped Olympus, three thousand meters high, and that night, not daring to waste the favorable wind, they crossed the Gulf of Thermaikos and ran past the Pallene peninsula, where, as Apollonius says, Cape Canastra rises out of the sea. Then they passed the second Chalcidic peninsula, Sythonia, and dawn gilded *Argo*'s sail under two-thousand-meter Mount Athos, at the head of the third peninsula, where today some two thousand Orthodox monks welcome pilgrims like me but not women, who have been banned here for almost a thousand years. Thus, with a

Myrina, Lemnos

favorable wind, in twelve hours *Argo* sailed some sixty nautical miles, which fits our estimate of five knots.

Now the wind died down again, and, carefully rounding vicious Cape Nymphaion, where Darius' fleet would be wrecked, the Argonauts rowed toward five-hundred-meter Mount Skopia, which beckoned them over the horizon to the island of Lemnos. They surely landed in cozy Myrina, which still bears the name of Queen Hypsipyle's mother. The Lemnian women had massacred all their men, except the queen's father, for paying more attention to the beautiful slave women they brought from Thrace than to their wives. Now these ferocious women prepared to fight off the Argonauts; but Lemnos was also the birthplace of Aphrodite's mischievous son Eros, and the women were soon in the arms of the sailors. Heracles alone sulked on the beach with a few henchmen and finally harangued his philandering comrades: Since his idea of glory is to repopulate Lemnos, let us leave Jason here and sail on, said he. Once again Jason was forced to weigh anchor against his will. In time, Queen Hypsipyle would bear Jason's son Euneus, who would reign over Lemnos when Agamemnon's expedition to Troy sailed by. Cautious like his father, Euneus' only contribution to the Trojan war would be a stock of the best wine of his island.

From Lemnos the Argonauts rowed the twenty nautical miles to Samothrace in eight hours, for an average of two and a half knots, which is again close to our estimate. There, they probably beached *Argo* in the bay of Paliopolis, which today is silted up. Samothrace is an island of goats, sulphurous waters, and magnetic stones, whose two-thousand-meter Mount Fengari (Moon Mountain) is visible from the Lemnian sanctuary of the Cabires, who initiated Orpheus into the mysteries that still seem to haunt Samothrace.

Another full day's rowing over the same distance brought *Argo* to the Chersonese, "with the Thracian coast to the left but leaving the island of Imbros to the right," says Apollonius, accurately describing the safest route. He also says that at dawn they stood ready to enter the bleak Hellespont as soon as the wind changed to the south, a correct description of the only condition that will allow a ship like *Argo* to sail into the eastern River of Ocean, where the prevailing current of about four knots is always adverse (we have seen why), except when the wind has blown plenty of water out into the Aegean and then veers to the south. Making the best of this rare piece of luck, by evening *Argo* had traversed the strait along the Roetian coast, past Ida, Dardania, Abydos, Percote, and Piteia, the men rowing and sailing at the same time, says Apollonius. In other words, they hugged the Asian shore just as modern yachtsmen do, and used their oars to keep the wind in their sails.

The following morning the Argonauts entered the broad Propontis, or Sea of Marmara, sailed past the mouth of the Aesepus River (today's Gönen), and beached *Argo* in the evening on the isthmus of Artake (today's Erdek). Until it was developed for tourism, this was a pleasant little port where gentle winds rustled the leaves of the olive trees, which watched over vineyards strewn with the ruins of the ancient capital. "On the Phrygian coast," says Apollonius, "there is a high peninsula whose isthmus barely surmounts the waves." He goes on to say that from the summit of Mount Dindimium one can see Thrace, the Mysian Mountains, and even the Bosporus. All true, and Alexander the Great had to build the isthmus up into a causeway in order to get his army onto Artake.

Here the Argonauts paid their respects to King Cizicus and got a good night's rest, after which they brought *Argo* around the peninsula to Chitus, which, Apollonius says, is also called Pandermos, "the cozy port." Its name (in Turkish Bandirma) means "wrapped in skins," and "wrapped in their skins and cloaks" is how the Argonauts slept on the beaches, says Apollonius.

Having made allies of King Cizicus and his Doliones by slaughtering the monstrous savages who periodically came down from the mountain, the Argonauts sailed on. But when a shift in the wind forced them back to Artake in the dark, the Doliones thought they were being invaded, and in the ensuing skirmish Cizicus lost his life. On hearing the news, his young queen, Cleite, hanged herself. Jason, who preferred not to leave enemies where he might have to call again on his way home, buried the king with full Greek honors and stayed another twelve days. Apollonius says that Tiphys exchanged his anchor stone for a heavier one, and still today, tourists are shown the Argonauts' abandoned stone anchor.

When Mopsus saw a hawk light on *Argo*'s sternpost, the Argonauts took their leave with a great sacrificial feast on the mountain and rowed away to the east, confident that Zephyrus would soon blow out of the west. But, despite the omen, Zephyrus was not eager to take over, and beyond the Rhyndacus River the oarsmen began to tire. Only Heracles rowed harder and harder, and finally broke his oar. At dusk *Argo* had to enter the harbor of Cius (today's Gemlik). Here the high mountains Apollonius mentions dominate Iznik, ancient Nicaea, where centuries later the Nicene Creed would be promulgated, and where the first Crusade would end in a shambles. While the Mysians feasted the Argonauts, Heracles looked for a spruce out of which to fashion a new oar, and Hylas, his pretty squire, wandered off to a stream and was spirited away by its nymph. Heracles refused to sail without him, and after a long wait and much debate, Jason decided to leave him behind; one has the feeling that he was glad to get rid of the superhero. In the end, Heracles went on to his own trials, presumably with Hylas.

Rounding Cape Poseidon (today's Boz Burnu), the Argonauts probably beached at today's Gebze; the distance is right, and so is the beach. Here King Amycus and his Bebryces met them with a challenge: no one could sail away from their beach until one of its members had beaten the burly king at fisticuffs. Jason, as usual, had the man, and taciturn Pollux put up his fists, punched the king over the ear, and split his skull. Then he wandered off into the night, brooding over what he had done, and never returned. The other Argonauts, untroubled by conscience, massacred the Bebryces and strewed their bodies "like logs" around the beach.

The following day *Argo* entered the narrow Bosporus and, thanks to helmsman Tiphys, rode out one of the sudden waves that still surprise these waters. Then, says Apollonius, where the strait makes a great curve to the right and just before the Black Sea comes into view, Notus again gave way to Boreas, the dominant north wind, and the ship sought shelter at the port of Phineus, the blind prophet. Today's Tarabaya, still marked Phinopolis on some old maps, is one of the best yacht basins in the Bosporus; it sits where the strait makes two broad curves, turns right at Büyükdere, and then runs straight into the Black Sea.

The gods, jealous of their monopoly, had condemned Phineus to a blind, hungry, and fetid existence because he had foreseen the future too clearly. Jason requested instructions for reaching Colchis, but the prophet offered his services on only one condition: the Argonauts must first rid him of the stinking Harpies who, at every meal, swooped down to claw the food out of his mouth. Again Jason had the team for the job. A great feast was prepared, and as soon as the batlike beat of the Harpies' wings was heard, Zetes and Calais, the sons of Boreas, took to the air. The first recorded aerial dogfight ended with the Harpies grounded on a distant isle, their lives spared only "because they were the hounds of Zeus." Grateful Phineus, bathed and fed, dared to warn Jason of the Clashing Rocks, which closed like jaws on anyone who tried to pass through the narrowest point in the strait. He advised him to send forward a dove so that the rocks would clash and part again just ahead of *Argo,* then to row like mad on top of the wave that would form before the rocks clanged shut once more. More than this, Phineus would not say; he had learned the hard way that, while men punish prophets who do not satisfy their expectations, gods punish those who poach on their perfect knowledge of the future. Nevertheless he did hint that the return route would be different.

The dove lost its tail feathers and *Argo* its sternpost, but the Argonauts made it through the rocks. Today, anchored to the bottom and surrounded by the "Devil's Currents," these rocks must still be watched carefully as one sails past Rumelikavaği, one of the narrowest stretches of the strait, guarded by Rumelihisari, "the castle on the Roman side," and Anadoluhisari, "the castle on the Anatolian side." Finally *Argo* rounded Apollonius' "Black Cape" (today's Kara Burnu), which in Turkish means exactly that. It is marked by what looks like a pile of dark tombstones, and beyond it lies the Black Sea, a schizophrenic body of water that cannot decide whether it belongs to the Mediterranean or the Caspian. Often sun-drenched and blue, with only a thin line of cloud on the horizon, it may at any moment be attacked by the north wind, which gallops out of the limitless steppes and transforms the thin cloud into the black shroud that surely gave the sea its name. For the Argonauts, it was an unknown sea, perhaps even a gulf of the Infinite Ocean.

At sight of the Black Sea, Jason hesitated, but Tiphys egged him on, and with Boreas on their port beam and the strange peaks of Colone (today's Alam and Chatal Dağ) to the south, they ran past the rivers Rehebas, today's Riva, and Filis, which flows into the sea at Ağva. But even brave Tiphys was tempted to turn back as the island of Thynias came into view, for it was topped by a huge apparition of Apollo; this is surely today the island of Kefken, still backed by strangely colored dunes from which Boreas sends columns of yellow dust high into the air under the shadow of Babi Dağ, "the Mountain of the Old Man."

The next day the rivers Calpe, which still bears the name, and Sangarius (today's Sakarya) were left behind, and as *Argo* reached the mouth of the river Lycus (today's Karasakar), the wind died and the Argonauts rowed to the beach under "high Cape Acherusias, where the river Acheron flows out of Hades' Cave in which silence never reigns, near flat stone reefs barely washed over by the waves," says Apollonius. Here King Lycus, the wolf, whose dominions stretched from this river to the Amazons' Thermodon, gratefully received the Argonauts who had rid him of his enemy Amycus, the boxer, and offered them his son as guide.

But Hades claimed his due: Idmon the seer was killed by a wild boar, and Tiphys, the incomparable helmsman, died of a fever. Around Heraklea (today's Ereğli), wild animals still abound, and in Kurbagali Deré (the gully of the frogs), huge caverns contain black pools whose frigid breath rustles the leaves that frame the caverns' entrances; and Apollonius' flat stone reefs are still visible beyond Baba Burnu, "the Old Man's Cape." I inquired if any Mycenean tombs had been found here, and an old man smiled and said, "When the Greeks were still here [before Kemal Atatürk], they showed me two tumuli on top of Baba

The sacred mountain

Burnu, which is now a military reservation." "We Turks," said Orham Duran, the local archaeologist, "we are hospitable Muslims . . . but war we like."

Jason's lamentations produced the new helmsman he needed: young Ancaeus, son of the sea god, whose knowledge of the stars would prove indispensable for the Argonauts' return. Zephyrus was blowing again, and *Argo* sailed past "the fertile lands of the Maryandini," Apollonius' accurate description of the only part of this coast that does not fall sheer into the sea. The Argonauts visited the tomb of Sthenelus, Heracles' comrade, whose ghost probably dazzled them, on the high rock that marks the entrance to the walled port of Amasra, ancient Sesamus. Then *Argo* sailed on to Cape Carambis "in a night and a day," almost a hundred nautical miles in twenty-four hours, a speed of just over four knots. This cape, says Apollonius, splits the wind, and today's Cape Kerempe, a name similar enough to Carambis, is famous for changes of wind; no sailor can tell if Boreas, when he strikes at Kerempe from the Crimea, will turn east or west. The Argonauts left Carambis at dawn, and by the time the sun had set and risen again they were safe behind Cape Sinop, having made a little less than their usual four or five knots. Sinop is a high peninsula rather like the Rock of Gibraltar, and here the Argonauts rested for twelve days and were joined by survivors of Heracles' expedition. Before sailing on from Sinop, they made the pilgrimage to Apollonius' "Sacred Mountain." No one could identify this mountain for me until through my binoculars I spotted an abandoned shrine, carved out of a hill off the road from Amasra to Kastamonu, some thirteen kilometers before Boyabat.

With Zephyrus brisk in their sail, the Argonauts passed the Halys River (today's Kizil Irmak), the "red river" that flows into the sea at Cape Bafra. Then they passed the Iris River (today's Yesil Irmak), the "green river" that flows into the sea at Cape Chiva. Apollonius calls these "the fertile deltas of the Assyrians," and the deltas of the two rivers are still the best lands for rice on this whole coast.

"The land of the Amazons," says Apollonius, "is watered by the hundred mouths of the river Thermodon," and from here on it is impossible to sail far without passing the mouth of a river. They all flow from behind the same coastal range, so the supposition that they all came from one great current is understandable. One of them is today's Terme, which the first illustrated Ptolemaic atlas (with maps by Crivelli, Bologna, 1477) clearly marks "Thermodontis F." Apollonius also says that the Amazons sacrificed on a black rock, and not far from here there is a second Kara Burnu, as black as the one we rounded to enter the Black Sea.

Ares' island and the hawk

The Argonauts had learned enough from the Lemnian women not to get involved with the Amazons, and without dallying they passed the land of the Chalybes, who, says Apollonius, spent their days digging and forging iron surrounded by soot, flames, and black smoke. This may well have been the West's first encounter with iron, and there is still plenty of coal for a forge along this coast. Next *Argo* rounded Zeus' Cape (probably today's Yasun Burnu, or "Jason's Cape"), whose greenish flanks topped with humid verdure shroud it in mystery, then ran along "the coast of the Tibureni" until the wind died down.

As the island of Ares, named for the god of war, came into view, a squadron of war birds launched an attack, and the Argonauts had to cover *Argo* with their shields. Finally they scared away the war god's birds by banging on their shields with their swords and swishing their helmet plumes in the air. No islands are marked on modern maps of this coast, but just beyond today's Giresun (ancient Keresos, where the Roman general Lucullus would discover cherries) and facing the mouth of Aksú Deresi stands a high rock out of whose wooded summit a pile of ruins shines white. Local tradition identifies them with the Temple of Mars, the Roman successor of Ares. As I stood near the mouth of the river, one falcon after another dropped out of the sky, and that evening at the inn, a man who carried a hooded falcon on his wrist told me proudly that this was where the best falcons come from. Ares' birds are not extinct.

Phineus had told Jason to put in at this inhospitable island for a pleasant surprise, and he was right. The descendants of Phrixus, who flew to Colchis on the golden ram, had been wrecked here while escaping from Aietes, King of Colchis, and after a little persuasion, the eldest, Argeus, agreed to join *Argo* and guide her to the land of the Golden Fleece.

With the wind in her sail, *Argo* passed a coast where, Apollonius says, savages made love in the open and took great care of the father while the mother was giving birth (Vespucci says the same about American Indians). It is a handsome coast, covered with hazelnut trees, here growing under a minaret, there under a Greek, a Roman, or a Byzantine ruin; and it is still studded with the small log huts that Apollonius describes and calls Mossines. Today's primitive Mossines still build them.

In a day and a night, says Apollonius, the Argonauts came to the cave where Cronos made love to the nymph Philyra and, caught in the act by his wife, Rhea, fled in the form of a stallion, leaving Philyra to give birth to Jason's tutor Cheiron, the centaur, half god, half stallion. Twenty-four hours at some six knots puts *Argo* at Trebizond (ancient Trapessos), one hundred and forty-four nautical miles away. Here the most likely cave for Philyra's ordeal is located under another military reservation (Turks love military reservations). At Trapessos, its trapezoid walls still framed in sunlit olive groves, the Comnenian Dynasty, the last Byzantine emperors, fleeing the Crusaders' sack of Constantinople, would complete the Byzantine millennium in 1461. And here Xenophon would march into the surf shouting "Thalassa!" (the sea!) after leading his ten thousand men all the way from Babylon.

Apollonius says that after leaving Philyra's cave the Argonauts ran along a coast peopled by many races, and after Trebizond the wooden Mossines are replaced by primitive stone dwellings, today surrounded by tea plantations. This is the rough land of the Lazes, a pre-Hellenic race that speaks a Turco-Georgian dialect. According to Turkish wags, the men spend all their time in mock feuds (*kan davas*) while their women do the work. Not so primitive!

At last the majestic Caucasus Mountains rose above the eastern horizon, and the Argonauts reached the far corner of the Black Sea, where legend says that Zeus' eagle pecked at the entrails of poor Prometheus, chained to the rock for stealing the gods' fire. As night fell, Argeus guided the Argonauts into the mouth of the Phasis River (today's Rioni), which flows into the sea at the Russian port of Poti. To their left stood Aia, the Colchian capital, and to their right stretched the plain of Ares, where a dragon as long as *Argo,* says Pindar, guarded the oak over which the Golden Fleece was draped, "flashing in the sun like Zeus' aegis." Mast and sail stowed, *Argo* glided silently into the rushes that framed the river's mouth. There the Argonauts dropped their stone anchor, and fell asleep.

V

MEDEA AND THE RIDDLE OF THE ARGONAUTS' RETURN

THE NEXT DAY crazy Idas goaded the reluctant Jason into demanding the fleece directly from King Aietes, son of Helios the Sun. The king reacted like Pelias, not refusing outright but stating impossible conditions. Jason would first have to yoke the king's two fire-breathing bulls and plow his field; then he would have to kill the dragon and sow its teeth; then he would have to slay the warriors who sprang from them. Fortunately for Jason, Eros' dart had pierced the heart of Aietes' young daughter Medea, her skin the color of the moon, her eyes like green wine, her hair aglow like a sunset. Apollonius' description of her sudden love is probably the first literary blush of romanticism, which would not bloom until the troubadours of southern France took it up more than fifteen hundred years later. It was Medea's love and the magic powers she obtained from her godmother, the great witch Hecate, always surrounded by the hissing of flames and the howling of dogs, that finally enabled Jason to pass all of Aietes' tests and claim the fleece. But the princess had betrayed her father, and in a blind fury, Aietes slaughtered Medea's elder sister.

Apollonius says that every wrong begets another. Medea herself would later have to watch Jason slaughter her brother, Ancaeus, and a series of horrors would gradually transform her from a loving maiden into a hateful witch, and Jason from a reluctant hero into a desperate vagabond.

Their mission accomplished, the Argonauts set fire to one of Aietes' fleets and, taking Medea with them, sailed for home. Phineus had told Jason that the return route would be different from the outbound route, and, in fact, to sail west along the whole length of the southern coast of the Black Sea is to buck prevailing winds and currents. Pindar suggests that the Argonauts emerged from Colchis directly into the Eastern (Indian) Ocean, sailed around to the Red Sea, then carried *Argo* for twelve days across a desolate land and came out into the Mediterranean through Triton's lake "in the land of Nile." Pindar considered the Caspian a gulf of ocean along whose shores one could reach the Red Sea, which of course it is not; to do this, the Argonauts would have had to escape Aietes up the Phasis River, carry *Argo* some one hundred and fifty kilometers up the Transcaucasian Valley to the Kura River, and finally sail down the Kura to the Caspian.

Apollonius comes closer to a practical route, but he includes a Homeric side trip that spoils everything. Once he gets the Ar-

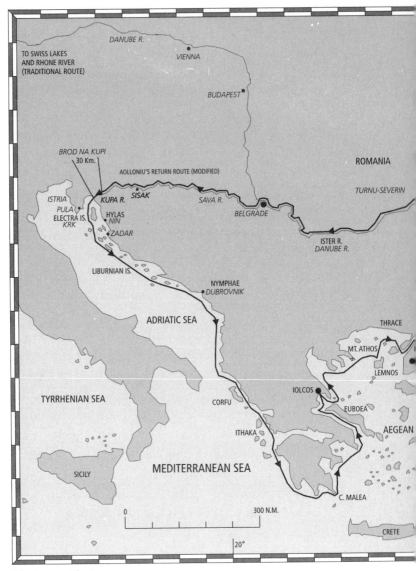

The Argonauts' return

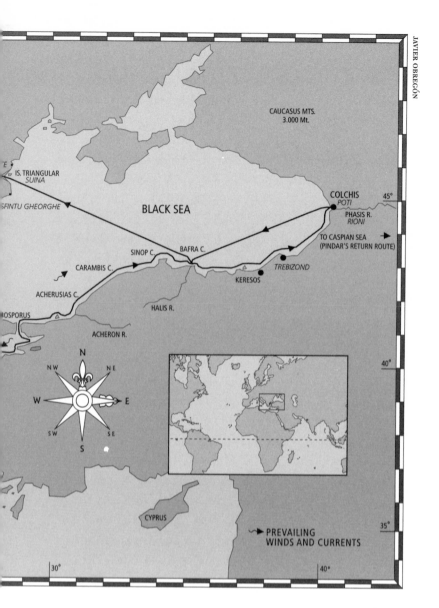

CAUCASUS MTS.
3.000 Mt.

IS. TRIANGULAR
SUINA

SFINTU GHEORGHE

COLCHIS
POTI

45°

PHASIS R.
RIONI

BLACK SEA

TO CASPIAN SEA
(PINDAR'S RETURN ROUTE)

SINOP C.   BAFRA C.

CARAMBIS C.

TREBIZOND

ACHERUSIAS C.

KERESOS

HOSPORUS

HALIS R.

ACHERON R.

40°

N

NW   NE

W   E

SW   SE

S

CYPRUS

35°

PREVAILING
WINDS AND CURRENTS

30°   40°

gonauts into the Adriatic, he makes them enter "Eridanus" (today's Po River, which Scylax considers to be another mouth of the Rhône), through the mouth of which, near Marseilles, he brings them back into the Mediterranean and the Tyrrhenian. From there he has them follow the route of Odysseus, complete with Circe, the Sirens, the volcano, the Floating Islands, and Scylla and Charybdis. Then he has them blown by Boreas from Cape Malea to Africa, exactly like Odysseus, there to get lost in Triton's lake and later to visit Crete. Finally he brings them home via Scheria, the land of fair Nausicaa. All this was apparently added by Apollonius in order to display his knowledge of Homer, and in fact the Alexandrians exiled him to Rhodes for plagiarism.

If we exclude Apollonius' side trip, his return route becomes credible. According to Apollonius, *Argo* began her homeward voyage by sailing west from Colchis only as far as the Halys River on Cape Bafra, some one hundred and seventy-five nautical miles. This would have taken less than twenty-four hours at the eight knots *Argo* could make with the godsent wind that Medea and Hecate surely conjured up for the first day of their flight, and Apollonius says that at the mouth of the river they paused to make sacrifices in honor of the witch. This done, they went back to real-life seamanship and, instead of continuing west along the coast against the prevailing winds, they headed northwest across the Black Sea to the mouth of the Ister (now the Danube). Here they put in at the "Triangular isle, Peuce," which the great river still forms between its two mouths at Santu Gheorghe and

Sulina, on the border of today's Romania. But here a nasty surprise awaited them. A squadron of Colchians led by Apsyrtus, Medea's younger brother, guarded the entrance to the river.

Jason, true to type, fell back on treachery. He vowed to surrender Medea and even to send Aietes the purple mantle of Queen Hypsipyle as a peace offering, and the young Colchian agreed to parlay at dusk. Unflinching, Jason slaughtered the youth and drank his blood as Medea watched. The Argonauts massacred the leaderless Colchians and, hearing that yet another Colchian squadron barred the Bosporus, sailed up the Danube and passed through a smoke-filled abyss, Apollonius' description of the famous Iron Gate of Turn-Severin, where the river rushes down a deep gorge at a speed of some fifteen knots. The Argonauts must have passed it by dragging *Argo* upstream.

Danubian tradition sends *Argo* all the way up the great river, then, with some sixty kilometers of portages, through Lakes Constance, Biel, Neuchâtel, and Leman, and down the Rhône to the Mediterranean. But at today's Belgrade, which is already five degrees north of Iolcos, the Danube takes a very definite turn northward, so that Jason and his navigator, Ancaeus, watching their home stars, would surely begin to worry about going too far north. The Sava River, on the other hand, runs into the Danube straight out of the west, and at Sisak the Kupa runs into the Sava, also out of the west. So I propose that the Argonauts must have sailed and rowed west up these rivers as far as Brod-na-Kupi, "the Kupa's Ford," where only thirty kilometers of hills dotted with lakes separated them from the Adriatic. Here, I think, the

Argonauts faced their only portage, a short but not an easy one, for the hills reach a height of three hundred meters. The feat is not impossible, however, if one remembers that in those days two things were plentiful that today are scarce: help, from the Celts, whom Apollonius mentions and who, in fact, were already there; and time, weeks or months of it, punctuated with sacrificial feasts. To this day, the city of Pula on the tip of the Istrian Peninsula prides itself on having been visited by the Argonauts.

So *Argo* was pushed over the hills on wooden rollers and joyfully returned to the brine below Istria. Then, according to Apollonius, the Argonauts sailed to the island of Electra, an island that today bears the unpronounceable name of Krk. Thence, says Apollonius, the Argonauts followed a river down to Hilas; and, in fact, from Krk to the south a chain of islands creates the river-like Podgorski or Velebitski Channel, which ends near Nin, whose ancient name could well have been Hilas, since this coast was peopled by the Hili, or Illyrians. Finally, south of Zadar, the Dalmatian coast begins to clothe its stones with olive and with cypress trees, and *Argo,* scenting home, sailed easily past the Liburnian islands to Nymphae (today's walled Dubrovnik), where there are still plenty of nymphs. The port used to be called Ragusa, possibly a corruption of *Argusa.* Finally, *Argo* made it home through familiar waters, around the Peloponnese and Cape Sounion, and up into the Gulf of Euboea, past Aulis, where later Agamemnon's fleet would gather to attack Troy and the king would sacrifice his daughter and earn his own death at the hands of her mother. But that is another story.

Word of the Golden Fleece and of red-haired Medea had

surely gone before them, and the Argonauts' entry into their beloved Gulf of Pagasae must have been a sight to see. But Medea had sunk into the evil that springs so easily from unrequited love, and having betrayed her own father and allowed her brother to be killed by Jason before her eyes, she now murdered Pelias and organized a feast at which she fed him to his daughters.

Jason, who in the end loved no one, decided to leave her and marry Glauce, the only daughter of Creon, King of Corinth, explaining to Medea that, having brought her from "the end of the world to the center of civilization," he had the right to seek his own royal destiny.

Her love now burning with a frozen flame, Medea gave Jason, as a wedding present for his new bride, the cloak she had made from the Golden Fleece. On the wedding day, when Glauce threw the resplendent cloak about her young shoulders, the fleece, leprous with so much treason, stuck to her flesh. When she tried to remove it, her flesh went with it and she died a horrible death.

Medea, no longer a sorceress but a full witch, cut the throats of the two children she had borne Jason and left for Athens with old King Aegeus. Aegeus was king of Athens at that time and Medea promised him a son. And Jason, the cautious prince, knowing at last that neither regal pomp nor human warmth was to be his lot, ended his days wandering in the frozen north. He was not the last whose false love transformed a maiden into a witch, or whose careful life ended in despair.

Nevertheless, the Argonauts had succeeded in extending the known world across the Black Sea, all the way to the Caucasus.

The river Phasis, they now thought, was the eastern River of Ocean, beyond which the Infinite Ocean roared around the back of the globe. And it would be up to Odysseus to discover where the western River of Ocean flowed from the other end of the Ocean into the known sea. "Time passes," says Pindar, "and sails fallen limp await the tremor of a new breeze."

VI

WESTWARD: THE ODYSSEY

IN THE GENERATION that followed *The Argonautica*, it was Odysseus' turn to push back the Infinite, this time westward from the strait of Tunis, where the island of Ogygia had thus far marked the end of the world, to the Pillars of Hercules at Gibraltar, gateway to the Infinite Ocean. But Odysseus, unlike Jason, was *politropon*, resourceful, and *peirates*, an adventurer, so the *Odyssey* is his story, not that of a team like *The Argonautica*. And his patron would be Athena, the goddess of intelligence.

Odysseus began his great voyage from Troy, and Homer's description of Troy led Heinrich Schliemann to discover it in 1870 on the southeast corner of the mouth of the Hellespont, and to wire the kaiser, "I have gazed upon the face of Agamemnon." After sacking and burning the city, Agamemnon and his brother,

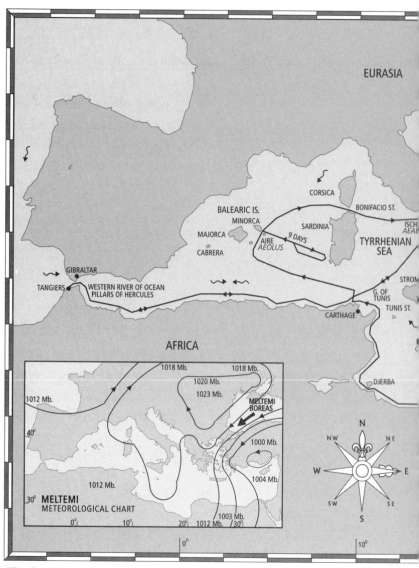

The odyssey

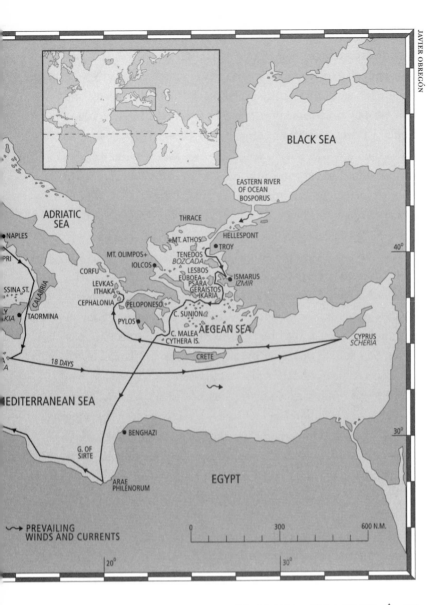

BLACK SEA

EASTERN RIVER
OF OCEAN
BOSPORUS

ADRIATIC
SEA

THRACE

+MT. ATHOS

HELLESPONT

NAPLES

PRI

MT. OLIMPOS+

TENEDOS
BOZCADA

TROY

IOLCOS

CORFU

LESBOS

EUBOEA

ISMARUS
IZMIR

SSINA ST.

LEVKAS
ITHAKA

PSARA
GERAISTOS

KIA

CALABRIA

CEPHALONIA

IKARIA

TAORMINA

PELOPONESO

PYLOS

C. SUNION

40°

A

C. MALEA
CYTHERA IS.

AEGEAN SEA

CYPRUS
SCHERIA

18 DAYS

CRETE

MEDITERRANEAN SEA

BENGHAZI

30°

G. OF
SIRTE

EGYPT

ARAE
PHILENORUM

PREVAILING
WINDS AND CURRENTS

0   300   600 N.M.

20°   30°

Menelaos, argued in front of their drunken troops about the return to Greece. Agamemnon decided to stay on the Trojan beach long enough to offer the proper sacrifices, but Menelaos, Nestor, Diomedes, and Odysseus ran their black ships into the surf and immediately made the short crossing to nearby Tenedos island (today's Bozcaada). From Tenedos, all except Odysseus sailed for Lesbos and thence directly to Geraistos at the southern end of the island of Euboea, one hundred and twenty nautical miles of open sea in twenty-four hours, a speed of five knots. They were in a hurry to get home before Boreas, which at the close of the *Iliad* blew on Patroclos' tomb, brought in the autumn storms.

For Odysseus, the opportunity of sacking one more Asian city and at the same time pleasing his commander in chief proved irresistible. Moreover, never frightened by men or gods but always respectful of the sea, he preferred to thread the southern Sporades and the Cyclades toward home rather than risk a storm in open water. So I submit that, after putting in again at the Trojan beach to pay his respects to Agamemnon, Odysseus led his squadron of twelve ships southward along the coast of Asia Minor—not north to Thrace, as tradition has it, which would have meant bucking the wind. And Homer tells us that when Odysseus sacked Ismarus (probably today's Izmir), the Cicones' inland allies counterattacked with war chariots, a typically Asian tactic.

Thence, after mourning his dead, Odysseus sailed with the freshening wind to the island of Ikaria and sat out the inevitable storm on its southeastern beach, which offers good shelter. When Boreas abated, he sailed from island to island across the Aegean to Cape Sounion, where his helmsman died and was buried with

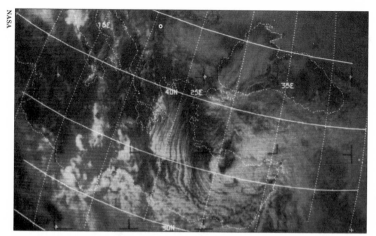

The meltemi

ceremony. His tomb must someday be found under the great temple that guards the setting sun. This duty done, the fleet tried to round Cape Malea, the highest of the Peloponnese "fingers," which even modern sailboats approach with caution. But Boreas (the meltemi) was up again, and though the Ithacans hastily struck their sails and rowed like mad toward land, they were blown past the island of Cythera to Africa and the land of the Lotus-Eaters.

The land of the lotus, probably a poppy, has traditionally been identified with the island of Djerba, but our meteorological map of the meltemi indicates that Odysseus may well have hit the African coast south of Benghazi, at the bottom of the Gulf of Sirte. This is closer to where Scylax placed the Lotus-Eaters; he calls the place Fontes Ammonii. I flew low along the coast of Tripolitania (Libya) looking for some likely place, and saw nothing but

The submerged port of the Lotus-Eaters, Arae Philenorum

snobbish camels and surprised nomads until I reached the bottom of the gulf. There I photographed a sunken port, clearly visible from the air. Unfortunately, I spotted no lotuses.

The meltemi sometimes blew Greek sailors to Egypt, and Menelaos fetched up there as he was taking his wayward Helen back to Sparta. So it is reasonable to suppose that Odysseus thought he was in Egypt. After lashing his drugged scouts under their benches, he rowed along the coast as long as it ran to the northwest in order to set sail for Greece from its northernmost point. Then, instead of sailing north from today's Benghazi, he awaited Notus in Carthage, and sailed north into the Gulf of Tunis.

There Notus, the sirocco, often turns suddenly into a tramontana (such a change sunk my catamaran off Spain, and I nearly got blown to Africa). It probably caught Odysseus in deep water, so he struck his sails and tried to row north toward the mountains of Sicily, which are not unlike those of the Peloponnese, but was slowly forced westward toward the Balearics, and not into the Tyrrhenian Sea, as tradition will have it.

We shall see that unless Odysseus reached the Balearic Islands, no sense can be made out of the rest of his voyage, and the island of Cabrera, off the southeastern coast of Majorca, is just like the island where Homer next describes the Ithacans feasting on the goats that give Cabrera its name. From here Homer says

Balearic Cave (Cave of the Cyclops)

that Odysseus could see the smoke of the fires of the Cyclopes, a race of cave dwellers who preferred not to work for their food. They would not be out of place in the caverns that pock the eastern coast of Majorca, whose mountains frame one of the most generously fertile plains in the whole of leisure-loving Spain, and I think it was in one of these caves, or better still of those of neighboring Minorca, that Odysseus and his scouts were trapped by the giant Polyphemus and escaped only after the Cyclops devoured half a dozen Ithacans. The wily Odysseus gave him undiluted wine and blinded him with a burning stake; and when the Cyclops rolled back the cave's stone door to let his sheep out to pasture, the surviving Ithacans escaped clinging to the fleece under the sheep's bellies.

Minorca is a land of stones where Hannibal raised his best slingshot warriors, and Homer tells us that the wounded giant tried to sink Odysseus' ship with a salvo of huge boulders. But Polyphemus' roar was drowned out by Odysseus' famous laugh, which still seems to ring around the great stone *navetas* that are strewn all over Minorca, shaped like upturned boats. Homer tells us that the Cyclopes were landlubbers, so the navetas are perhaps mementos of the victorious Ithacans' ships.

The squadron next sailed to the island of Aeolus, king of the winds. In front of the port of Mahón, the Minorcan capital, there is an island called Isla del Aire, the "Isle of the Wind," whose higher coast, gilded by the setting sun, reminds one of Homer's "coast of bronze," while its other coast sinks into the sea as if the winds were going to send it down into the deep. Here Aeolus gave Odysseus the zephyr he needed to sail home, and a leather pouch that was not to be opened. For nine days the fleet sailed east; Odysseus never rested until, in the morning mists, he thought he saw his home islands. Then, exhausted, he fell asleep, and immediately Eurylochus, the ship's troublemaker, opened Aeolus' leather bag, thinking it might be full of gold. Out leaped Euros, the east wind, and the hapless fleet was blown back to Aeolus, who refused to have anything further to do with its godforsaken crew.

The Isle of the Wind (Aeolus' floating isle)

Odysseus now knew approximately which way he had to row for home, but after rowing two hundred and fifty nautical miles in six days, at an average speed of just under two knots, he came up against the barrier formed by Corsica and Sardinia. Looking for a way through, he found the Strait of Bonifacio, where the port of the same name, with its high and narrow entrance, answers exactly to Homer's description of Telepylos, the port of the Laestrygones. Tradition has always placed it here but has never explained why Odysseus should have passed westward through the strait if he came out of the Tyrrhenian Sea, when he obviously knew he should be heading east. Bringing him from the Balearics is the only way to solve the problem.

The Bard tells us that in Telepylos "sunrise and sunset follow each other so closely that if a man did not need sleep, he could earn double wages as a herdsman and as a shepherd too," a statement that has given rise to all sorts of conjectures. Some have sent Odysseus far enough north for him to discover the midnight sun, while others have sent him south to the Canary Islands, where he might have noticed the shortened twilight of the tropics. Neither solution makes sense, but the fact is that on Corsica, as on Minorca, sheep often shelter from the sun in caves, and the shepherd who leads them out to pasture in the cool evening meets the cowherd bringing his cattle home for the night to be milked in the early morning. So, if one wished, one could do both jobs, and "earn double wages."

The fleet sought shelter inside the deep port of Bonifacio, but Odysseus preferred to moor his own ship to a rock near a cave outside the harbor's mouth, clearly visible in our photograph. As usual, he was right, for the Laestrygones turned out to be vicious giants who bombed the trapped fleet with huge rocks hurled down from their city high above the port, and only Odysseus' ship escaped. From here on he would have to depend on his own wits, and on a series of women, sorceresses, and nymphs who would both help and hinder him.

Bonifacio (the Laestrygones' port)

Odysseus' lonely ship next reached Aeaea, the island of the sorceress Circe, King Aietes' younger sister. Monte Circeo on the Italian coast east of Bonifacio has usually been identified with Aeaea, but Homer leaves no doubt that Circe lived on an island. By watching the passage of his home stars, Odysseus probably knew that from Bonifacio he must sail south of east to reach home, so I think he made his landfall on the island of Ischia to the southeast. It was known of old as Aenaria, a name not unlike Aeaea, and it was also called Pithekoussai, the isle of the apes, which fits Homer's description of an island full of wild animals. That the name has moved from the coast to a neighboring island need not worry us: historical names are nomads.

Spotting a column of smoke, Odysseus sent Eurylochus with a patrol to investigate, and the troublemaker, having learned prudence at Telepylos from his captain, stayed outside while his men entered Circe's castle. They were immediately transformed by the sorceress into wild pigs. Eurylochus ran back to the beach and strongly suggested leaving right away; but Odysseus, who had been forced to abandon his fleet at Telepylos, refused to leave his men in the hands of Circe, perhaps not only out of loyalty but because the presence of a woman, sorceress or not, interested him. He marched to Circe's castle, and on the way Hermes, his forebear, intercepted him and gave him the magic herb he needed in order to recover his scouts and to make Circe his for a year. During this time, young Elpenor got drunk, fell off Circe's roof, and broke his neck, and several Mycenean tombs have in fact been found on Ischia, one of them topped by a wine jug.

Circe did everything possible to retain her Ithacan lover, but she finally released him on one condition: he must first sail to the River of Ocean "where the sun goes to its death," there to consult with the dead; then she would give him the choice of two routes for home. The northeast wind would take him west, she said, and the River of Ocean's current would start him back. In fact, along the North African coast the summer winds tend to blow out of the east, and we have seen why the surface current in the Strait of Gibraltar runs back into the Mediterranean.

Homer's description of the stony beach on which Odysseus landed, the tall forests through which he passed, and the volcanic caverns that were the antechamber of the entrance to Hades all indicate that Odysseus reached the western extreme of his journey near today's Tangiers. Thus he reached the end of the western Mediterranean and discovered that, like Jason's Black Sea, it was not a gulf of Infinite Ocean but a finite sea into which the eastern River of Ocean flowed.

The Odyssey's Book of the Dead is an emporium of legends, only a few of which we can note here. As soon as Odysseus poured sacrificial blood into the great ditch, his mother, Anticleia, rose to give him his first news of home, reviving his desire to return and wreak vengeance on the impudent suitors who occupied his palace and pursued his wife, Penelope. The seer Teiresias warned Odysseus of trials ahead, and prophesied that he would die a peaceful death by the sea. Finally, the shades of Agamemnon and Achilles both offered Odysseus advice. The commander in chief, murdered by his wife's lover, warned him not to trust anyone, not even his wife; and Achilles, hailed by Odysseus as the greatest of all those who had died at Troy, answered, "Odysseus, my lord, spare me your praise of death. I would rather be the slave of a pauper, but alive, than prince of all these ghosts." Greeks have always loved life above all else.

The passage of time gradually focuses legends into ever clearer history, and Homer's account of Odysseus' return is much more precise than the accounts of the Argonauts' voyage home. Once the current of the River of Ocean had brought Odysseus back into the Mediterranean, he had no trouble sailing east again to Circe's island, thanks to the fact that in winter the wind along the North African coast tends to reverse itself. Circe then told him how to start for home: after avoiding the sirens, he should choose between two routes. If he took the first he would pass a fiery island "where even Zeus' doves dare not fly," then enter a dangerous strait; the second would require navigating the "Floating Islands" and sailing around the triangular isle.

His men, their ears plugged with wax, rowed Odysseus past the Sirens, who probably sunbathed as Sirens still do on the

Capri (the Sirens' isle)

CRISTINA MARTINEZ DE IRUJO DE OBREG

beach in Capri. According to tradition, Odysseus was tied to the mast, but it is more likely that he was tied to a bench, since the mast would surely have been stowed for maximum speed while rowing. Then, following the Italian coast down to Cape Vaticano, Odysseus easily picked the more seamanlike of the two routes described by Circe: not via the Floating Islands (the Eole) and eastward around Sicily, but past Stromboli's volcano and through the strait that separates Scylla from Charybdis, at today's Messina. Hugging the Calabrian shore, as recommended by Circe (and by modern sailing directions), he avoided Charybdis to the west, where even today small boats must be careful of whirlpools known as *garofolli*. But the price of his seaman's caution was high: six of his men were taken by Scylla, the giant octopus that guarded the eastern shore.

Thus, thanks to Circe's precise instructions, Odysseus was finally on the way to rounding the Italian "barrier" that had been keeping him from home. But, Homer says, there were clouds over Scylla, and even today clouds over Calabria announce a sirocco. Once he was through the strait, the south wind forced Odysseus to land on Trinacria, the Sun God's island (certainly Sicily), triangular and dominated by the sun. The best rangeland on the island lies north of Taormina's beach, where, I believe, Odysseus must have landed to take his rest. Here Eurylochus convinced the hungry crew that the Sun God's cattle, which Circe had warned Odysseus not to touch, were for eating.

Awakening too late, Odysseus hurriedly set sail, but the god's revenge was swift. Off the southeast tip of Sicily the sky darkened while the winds clashed, and, enveloped in "lightning and the smell of sulphur," Odysseus' ship was lost with all hands, the helmsman's skull split by the falling mast. Only Odysseus survived, clinging to a raft he improvised by lashing the mast to the keel with a leather stay.

First he was blown back to the strait, but Boreas soon returned and blew his raft south to Ogygia (today's Malta), which, before the Ithacans entered the western Mediterranean, was thought to be the end of the world. There Calypso, the lonely nymph, kept him captive and gave him two sons. After seven years, Zeus, persuaded by Athena, sent Hermes to order Calypso to help her lover build a boat and to give Odysseus precise navigational instructions. He must sail dead east by the sun, keeping the Big Dipper on his left at night, "the only constellation," in her words, "which never bathes in Ocean's stream." Homer's description of the boat (not as tradition holds, a raft) has helped us to reconstruct *Argo,* and the sailing directions will serve to propose where Homer must have lived.

In his hand-built boat, Odysseus, alone, sailed east for eighteen days, the longest leg of the Odyssey. He traveled toward Scheria, which, according to Homer, was a land distant not only from Ogygia, Calypso's island, but also from Ithaca. Eighteen days and nights sailing east from Malta at an average of two and a half knots, a reasonable speed for a small, improvised, and single-handed sailboat, would carry Odysseus about a thousand nautical miles east. That would bring him to Cyprus; and Homer's description of the zephyr that caressed Scheria's orchards fits Cyprus well. Apollonius calls Scheria Drapane "the Sickle," a good name for this gracefully curved island, where I place the home of Navsicaa "of the white arms."

On the way, Zeus' brother Poseidon, who hated the Ithacan for having blinded his son Polyphemus, spotted the lonely sailboat and raised a terrible storm, which sank Odysseus' boat. But once again, a nymph and a goddess were ready to rescue him. The nymph Io protected Odysseus with her veil, and Athena guided him onto the Phaeacian shore, whose description in Homer fits that of western Cyprus. The river mouth near Paphos' two harbors allowed Odysseus to swim past the reefs Homer describes and to come ashore near the "double harbor," where Aphrodite was born. Here Navsicaa, who was playing ball on the beach "more graceful than Delos' tall palmtree," rescued the exhausted hero and led him to her father's palace after telling him on the way how to gain the king's favor and how to make an ally of the queen.

King Alcinous, knowing a hero when he saw one, feasted and entertained his guest with the songs of a blind bard, whom tradition has consecrated as Homer's self-portrait. Fascinated, Alcinous listened to Odysseus' story, and even organized games in his honor. But since Odysseus would not stay, he finally agreed to send him home in a ship manned by fifty princes and loaded with gifts of copper, the metal that gave Cyprus its name. The ship, said Alcinous, needed no helmsman, which suggests that the Phaeacians may have introduced the West to the East's lateen sail, with which it would be possible to sail from Cyprus to Ithaca in a steady meltemi with a steering oar lashed at the proper angle, just as Joshua Slocum, the first and the greatest of the lone circumnavigators, crossed the Indian Ocean with a lashed tiller in a steady monsoon.

Be that as it may, it was on Cyprus that great-hearted Odysseus left a corner of his heart. Timidly, Navsicaa had declared her love for him, and Alcinous had showed how much he would welcome the Ithacan for his daughter. But Odysseus would only vow never to forget the maiden to whom he owed his life, and insisted on returning home. Navsicaa possessed a rare virtue; she loved but let live. So, after a twenty years' absence, Odysseus returned to Ithaca.

The identity of Ithaca has caused endless arguments, mainly because of Odysseus' statement that it was the island that sloped most to the west. It seems clear to me that Odysseus referred to the fact that the steeper of Ithaca's two long coasts slopes west.

Ithaca's steep coast

Today's Itháki is as steep as Odysseus' son, Telemachus, said it was when he refused Melenaos' gift of horses because there was no room on Ithaca for them to graze; and Itháki's rivals, the neighboring islands of Levkás and Cephalonia, both have good pasture.

Telemachus had gone to search for news of his father, and the suitors, who wished Odysseus dead and vied for the hand of his rich widow, laid an ambush for Telemachus. In front of Polis there is a rocky islet (today's Deskalio), which may well have been Homer's Asteris. It sits in the channel separating Itháki from Cephalonia, and on Cephalonia, well hidden behind Deskalio, lies a deep blue inlet bearing the name Paleokaravos "the Ancient Ship," which could have served for the suitors' ambush. But Telemachus outflanked his enemies by sailing up the eastern coast of Ithaca. On the northeastern shore of Itháki itself, just over the island's high narrow spine, there is another good harbor, Frikes, and Kalamos, an easy walk for Odysseus from Polis and for Telemachus from Frikes, fits Homer's description of the site where father and son were reunited at the Hut of Eumaeus, the faithful swineherd.

How Odysseus, disguised as a beggar, vanquished the suitors, is surely one of the most exciting "finales" ever written, but we cannot recount it here. Odysseus' most important feat had still to be accomplished. Twenty years had left their mark on him, and, still in his beggar's disguise, he did not find it easy to convince Penelope that he really was her husband. Neither maiden, nymph, nor sorceress, Penelope was a real woman of flesh and blood who had kept the suitors waiting for twenty years with her weaving and unraveling, and she had to be won.

Sailing to the island of Ithaca, I anchored in Sant Andrea, traditionally identified as Odysseus' harbor, but when the south wind made up, Sant Andrea proved unsafe. So we sailed on to Polis, in the north of the island, a much safer harbor for the king of Ithaca. There I rowed across the bay to a cavern where fragments of copper tripods had been found, tripods like those that Odysseus hid in a cave as soon as he returned to Ithaca. Then I climbed the herb-scented hill to Stávros, where I could see Frikes as well as Polis, two perfect ports from which Odysseus and his son Telemachus could meet at the hut of Eumaeus, on the ridge that separates the two harbors. At the magic hour when the sea stills its sighs so that the song of the cicada can chant the evening's dying, I knew that the remains of Odysseus' palace must one day be found under the terraced vineyards I had climbed. Its stones would surely still be stained with the blood of the suitors massacred by father and son in the "grand finale" of the greatest of adventure stories. Here Teiresias' prophecy would be fulfilled, and Odysseus' life would end like an autumn sunset, aglow with the love of Penelope, of Telemachus, and of the people of Ithaca, on the luminous ridge where a few tall cypresses still guard his olive groves and his vines.

VII

EAST TO THE ISLES OF SPICE

W HEN ALEXANDER THE GREAT invaded the Asian continent and crossed the Oxus and the Indus, his ambition was to reach the Ganges, and so perhaps to sail into the Ocean Sea. But his exhausted troops mutinied and forced him to march southward across the desert, then to sail back to the Persian Gulf in the coastal vessels of Admiral Nearcos. Not even a demigod could reach the Oriental boundary of the known landmass, and eight centuries had to pass before the Muslims, "God's subjects," finally reached the shores of the Infinite Ocean.

Muhammad, the Prophet, was born in the year A.D. 570 in the city of Mecca, on Jazirat al Arab, the "Arabian Island," bounded by two seas and a desert. Hagia Sophia, the most impressive church in all Christendom, had but recently been consecrated in

Constantinople; England's conversion to Christianity was beginning; the Visigoths were still conquering Spain; and Buddhism had just been brought to Japan. Muhammad received his first divine revelation on Mecca's Mount Hira, when he was forty years old, and his wife Kadija, older and wealthier than he, believed

The Great Mosque of Mecca, with the Kaaba

from the first in his One God "who created man and teaches him everything through the Scriptures." A wife who believes in a man's vocation is priceless, and thanks to Kadija, the Prophet kept his faith during the two long years he had to wait for the

Archangel Gabriel to resume his revelations. But monotheism did not suit the idolatrous merchants of Mecca, and in the year A.D. 622, Muhammad and his few disciples had to emigrate to Yathrib, today's Medina al Nabi, "the Oasis of the Prophet," some three hundred kilometers to the north. There they founded their first mosque, and from this exodus, or *Hegira*, the Muslim calendar began to count its years.

The archangel ordered the Prophet to wage war on infidels; the Muslims began by attacking the annual caravan from Damascus and ended by defeating the Meccans who besieged Medina. During the next six years, tribe after tribe of Bedouins joined the victors, and in A.D. 628 Muhammad returned to Mecca at the head of ten thousand men to banish the idols from the Kaaba, the black "House of God," which today marks the center of Islam in the great Mosque of Mecca, visited every year by some two million pilgrims. There, according to the Koran, God promised Abraham a son, and while his wife, Sarah, was still childless, his Egyptian slave Hagar gave birth to Ishmael. God then commanded Abraham to sacrifice Ishmael, but at the last moment allowed him to substitute a lamb. The Bible, on the other hand, says that it was in Jerusalem that God commanded Abraham to sacrifice Sarah's son Isaac, then allowed him to substitute a ram. Consequently, Mecca is the center of Islam and Jerusalem of Israel, and Arabs trace their descent to Ishmael, while Jews trace theirs to Isaac. Today's enemies are blood brothers who share the story of Abraham's submission to God.

Before the Sharia, Muslim's legal code, limited marriages to four, the Prophet consolidated his power by means of a dozen matrimonial alliances, and in the year A.D. 632, after proclaiming his last revelation to the faithful on the plain of Arafat, he died in the arms of his favorite wife, Aysha, and was buried in Medina.

Aysha's father, Abu Bakr, who became the first caliph, consolidated Islam by subduing the remaining rebel tribes and toppling their false prophets. Omar, the second caliph, invaded the two great neighboring empires, Persia and Byzantium, and from there Islam proceeded to consume the known world as if driven by the four winds. Today its five basic precepts—faith, prayer, alms, fasting, and pilgrimage—guide the lives of more than seven hundred and fifty million people from Indonesia to Guinea and from Russia to Madagascar.

Three qualities made the Muslims invincible: the mobility of their warriors, almost as easy to supply as their camels and mules; the constant presence of God, which gave their "holy war" a sharpened sense of destiny; and their God-fearing clemency for the vanquished. It is said that when Sofronius, the silk-clad patriarch of Jerusalem, walked solemnly out of the city's gates on a red carpet to surrender, the Muslim general, on his dusty camel, exclaimed: "Allah be praised; are these the men who have resisted us?" But the Koran says: "Believe in God, and in what He revealed to Abraham, Ishmael, Isaac, Jacob, Moses, Jesus, and the Prophets: make no distinction between them, and submit only to Him," and the Hadith, which with the Sharia completes Muslim written tradition, says, "When you die, your neighbors will ask what goods you have left; but the Angel will ask what good you have done." Islam does not complicate matters: no original sin, no monasticism, no monogamy, and no charging interest on money. So in an age of schisms, Jews and Christians did not find it hard to accept a religion that believed in one God and placed Moses and Jesus among its prophets, and Jews who did not convert were allowed to live in peace as long as they paid the annual tax of one day's wages plus a measure of wheat.

In A.D. 642, Islam turned west, invaded Egypt, and occupied Alexandria. The Byzantine fleet, which was still afloat, was annihilated off Licia, and in 682, General Uqbah Ibn Nafi occupied Tripoli, Carthage, and Tangiers, the last Byzantine naval bases. The Muslims reached the Atlantic at Agadir and became masters of the southern Mediterranean. But, on the beach at Agadir, Ibn Nafi rode his charger into the Atlantic surf and proclaimed, "God is my witness that only the ocean has put a limit on what I have conquered in His name." He did not notice that the wind blew the foam west across the ocean.

The Muslims turned south across the Sahara, a sea of sand, which they navigated as if it were the Mediterranean. Then they ran down the West African coast at least as far as Cape Verde, where in his map of 1500 Juan de la Cosa placed the crescent moon. They also turned north, and in 711, Tariq Ibn Ziyab landed on Gibraltar (Djeb-al-Tar, Mount Tariq). His Moors defeated King Rodrigo's Visigoths near Cadiz, cornered the Christians in the mountains of northern Spain, and penetrated into France, where they were finally stopped at Tours in 732 by Charles Martel, Charlemagne's grandfather. In the meantime, Abu Qasim occupied Samarkand, where Tamerlane (*timur* means "eastern," and *lan,* "lame") lies buried, and Tashkent. He crossed the Oxus and the Indus, and established Islam first in

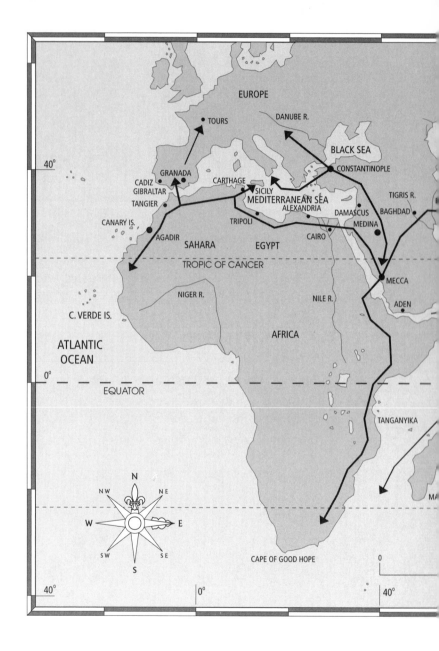

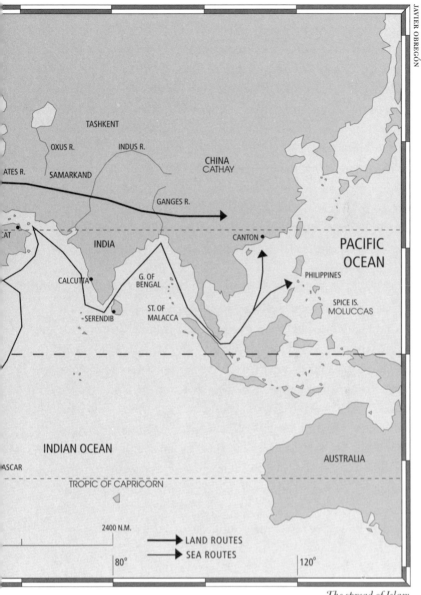

TASHKENT

OXUS R.   INDUS R.

ATES R.   SAMARKAND

CHINA
CATHAY

GANGES R.

AT

INDIA

CANTON

PACIFIC
OCEAN

CALCUTTA

G. OF
BENGAL

PHILIPPINES

SERENDIB

ST. OF
MALACCA

SPICE IS.
MOLUCCAS

INDIAN OCEAN

AUSTRALIA

ASCAR

TROPIC OF CAPRICORN

2400 N.M.

LAND ROUTES

SEA ROUTES

80°   120°

The spread of Islam

India and then on the frontiers of Cathay. "Always seek knowledge," says the Koran, "even in China."

The expansion of Islam to the ends of the Eurasian continent gave rise to an interminable series of wars of succession, principally between Sunnis and Shiites; and also to all sorts of heresies, such as that of the *hashshashin,* or assassins, who, drugged with hashish, spread terror in the name of Islam during the eleventh and twelfth centuries. Their peaceful descendants, the Ishmaelites, today limit themselves to paying the Aga Khan a tribute equivalent to his weight in diamonds. In A.D. 671, Islam's capital passed from Mecca to Damascus, where the exploits of the legendary Bedouin hero Antar, which so inspired medieval Europe, are still recited in public; in 762 it passed to Baghdad, where Haroun al-Raschid enjoyed the Thousand and One Nights; finally, in 973 it passed to Cairo, today the capital of Islam.

Islamic culture reached its zenith in Spain, where the Muslims stayed for almost eight centuries, embroidering the Spanish language with more than four thousand Moorish words, adorning the austere peninsula with jewels like the university mosque at Córdoba and the Alhambra at Granada, and inspiring heroes who, like El Cid in the eleventh century, took the field as often for the Moors as against them. When in 1492 the Catholic sovereigns completed the reconquest by taking Granada, the defeated Moorish king Boabdil was not the only one who wept. Andalusian song and poetry still weep for the heyday of Islam: "Weep not for your robe, daughter of Bakili," says a Muslim song, "or the river will carry away your youth. Come into the shade, and I will weave for you a robe more precious than the one you have lost, a robe made of caresses."

Islam means submission to God, and in this sense it is synonymous with our word *enthusiasm,* which comes from the Greek *en theos,* "possessed by God." And it is enthusiasm, perhaps more than any other emotion, that identifies the Renaissance with antiquity and distinguishes both from the Middle Ages. It also distinguishes the West, where the quest for God is pursued with enthusiasm, from the East, where God is sought in withdrawal. Consequently, Islam's enthusiasm places it squarely at the source of the Renaissance of the West, and as soon as it found the leisure to absorb the cultures it had conquered, it became the bridge by which the West rediscovered its ancient heritage. "The most sublime homage that can be offered to God is to know His work," wrote Averroes, and the combination of Arab enthusiasm with the cultures of Egypt, Greece, Persia, India, and Byzantium produced a constellation of artists and scientists who reaped the wisdom of the ancient world, cultivated it during Europe's Middle Ages, and passed it on to the European Renaissance.

In the seventh century the Arabs revived the library of Alexandria, and in the eighth, Abu Masa Dshafar crowned his chemical research with the discovery of *aqua regia* (nitric and hydrochloric acids). In the ninth, while Ptolemy's *Geography* was being translated into Arabic, Mohammed Ibn Musa al-Kwarismi invented algebra, confounding generations of students (our word *algorithm* comes from *al-Kwarismi*). In the tenth century, while the University of Córdoba was being founded in the famous mosque, al-Hazan codified the laws of physics, and al-Sufi, in his *Book of Stars,* mentioned nebulae, those unseen galaxies that the seventeenth century would have to rediscover. In the eleventh, while the crypt of Chartres was being built, Ibn Sina (Avicenna) wrote the canon that dominated Western medicine for centuries. And during the eleventh and twelfth centuries, even before the troubadours sang their first love songs in France, Omar Khayyám, a mathematician and astronomer who lived to be almost one hundred, composed one of the most romantic of poems, the *Rubaiyát;* Ibn Rushd (Averroes) wrote his commentaries on Plato and Aristotle; and Mohammed Idrisi drew the first complete map of Eurasia. In the thirteenth century, while Genghis Khan led the Mongols west, while the alcazar was being built in Seville, and while Saint Francis preached in Assisi, Yaqut wrote his *Geographic Encyclopedia.* And in the fourteenth, when the Swiss Confederation was being formed, the Black Death was ravaging Europe, and the Alhambra was being built in Granada, Ibn Battutah's description of his voyages earned him the title of the Muslim Marco Polo, and Ibn Khaldun wrote a history not unworthy of Herodotus.

From the ancient Greeks, Islam inherited the astrolabe and from the Chinese the compass, which the Muslims improved by introducing a free-swinging magnetic needle instead of a floating card. With the astrolabe they measured the angular height above the horizon of the sun and stars, but since the astrolabe finds its horizon by hanging freely, it is not an easy instrument to use on a pitching ship; so, for shipboard use, the quadrant supplanted it (see page 122), and a rudimentary form of the quadrant, the *kamal,* is still used by Muslim sailors. The quadrant can be held firmly in one hand while it is aimed at a star. In the instant when the star is lined up, the string from which the weight hangs is pressed against the scale with the other hand, so that the angle can be read at leisure. (I have measured the height of the polestar within two degrees with a reproduction of a fifteenth-century quadrant.) Of course, to "shoot" the sun one does not risk one's retina by aiming the instrument directly at it; one simply lines up the shadow of the foresight with the backsight. These basic instruments, like so much else, came to the west via Islam, and without them, discovery could never have gone much further.

Islam also developed a ship so fast and so maneuverable that it compares favorably with the Portuguese caravel, which spread to Spain and was essential to the discovery of America. Like the Polynesians' praus, the dhow's teak

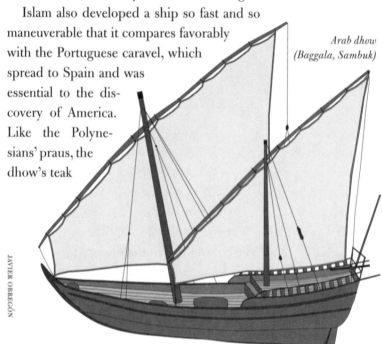

Arab dhow (Baggala, Sambuk)

timbers were originally lashed together with ropes made of twisted coconut fibers, then pounded with wooden hammers, the holes filled with coconut fiber mixed with a paste made of tree gum and lime. Iron nails were not used until later because it was thought they might be pulled out by underwater magnetic forces. Most important, the Arab dhows were lateen-rigged, and their

The Isles of Spice

spars, which were as long as the hull and might weigh over a ton, could be spread to run with the wind or raised to shape the sail into a high triangle in order to sail relatively close to the wind, much closer than any square sail could.

It was with these instruments and ships that the Muslims first dominated the Mediterranean. They then learned to ride the southwest monsoons in summer and the northeast monsoons in winter, in order to establish trade routes from the Arabian peninsula east by way of Calicut and the Malay straits to Canton in

China, and south to Tanganyika and Madagascar. Eventually, they sailed on to the Spice Islands, a quarter of the way around the world, where they established the monopoly that lasted until the Portuguese also learned to follow the monsoons and established their *factorías*, or trading forts. The spice trade was essential to the expansion of Islam, for Europe was as addicted to spices as it was to gold and silver. Spices were supposed to preserve meat, though in fact they only disguised its decay; and they were supposed to cure many ills and to serve as aphrodisiacs, a fallacy surely fostered in their rich lovers by Renaissance beauties.

Sailing down the African coasts, the Muslims were the first to

The constellations of Sagittarius and Leo, by a Muslim artist (Samarkand)

cross the equator; that is why many important stars near the equator and south of it have Arab names, not Greek or Latin ones, as in the north. It seems, in fact, that the Muslims may even have sailed down to the Cape of Good Hope before Europe knew it existed. After a long search for a map that is mentioned in

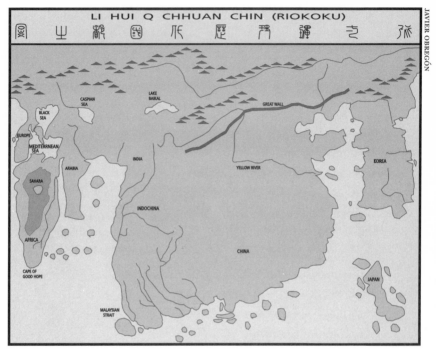

LI HUI Q CHHUAN CHIN (RIOKOKU)

图 里 龢 国 氒 歷 再 譚 己 承

JAVIER OBREGÓN

The Kangnido (1402)

Joseph Needham's great work *Science and Civilisation in China,*
I found the Kangnido, a Sino-Korean map of 1402, where the in-
formation is mostly Muslim and Africa is drawn with a cape al-
most three generations before Bartolomeu Dias rounded the
Cape of Good Hope, before Henricus Martellus made the first
European map where Africa is properly drawn, and before
seventy-year-old Ahmed Ibn Najid led Vasco da Gama to India.
Interestingly, the curator of the Ryukoku University's library in
Kyoto agreed to give me a colored photograph of the carefully

guarded map, but when I asked him for some black-and-white details he refused, reminding me that this was a Buddhist treasure of which I was the only westerner to own a complete copy. Oriental views of research are different from ours. In any case, the Chinese certainly did not round the cape, though their great navigator, Chung-Ho, a Muslim, made it to Arabia and probably even to East Africa. So the existence of the cape can only have been transmitted to the Chinese by the Muslims.

Nevertheless, wealth, culture, and science alone are not enough to spark the instinctive leap that great discoveries require. In the east, the Muslims were content to coast from the Bay of Bengal to the Isles of Spice, and in the west to turn north into Spain and south across the Sahara. On the shores of the Atlantic and on the islands that look out onto the Pacific, the Muslims of the endless desert and of the endlessly repeated arabesques respected the Infinite Ocean, which they called the Sea of Darkness, and confined themselves to the coastal navigation they had learned from the Greeks. With their lateen sails they could have tacked from island to island into the Pacific, and, even more eas-

The Cape of Good Hope today

ily, they could have sailed into the Atlantic from Cape Verde, where the trade winds blow constantly toward America. But they never ventured beyond Eurasia, not even westward to the Canary Islands, nor, at the other end of the world, eastward beyond the Philippines, where Muslims still fight Christians today. There, in the sixteenth century, Magellan's fleet met Moors who spoke Spanish; Elcano says so in his diary, which I found, again after much searching, in the Indiferente General of the Archive of Seville.

Ibn Nafi was right; Islam's limits were set by the ocean, but in the meantime, another nation was making indispensable contributions to the naval knowledge of the West.

VIII

WEST TO VINLAND

T HROUGHOUT THE MIDDLE AGES, the Vikings, who took
their name from their Norwegian fjords, or *viks,* spread terror in their slim warships from Scandinavia to Sicily and from
Ireland to the great rivers of Russia, while their peasant brothers,
the Norsemen, followed their fortune in beamy *knarrs.* Vessels of
both types were recovered from Roskilde Fjord near Skuldelev,
Denmark, in 1968. One of these ships is at Viking Ship Hall in
Oslo; it was brought from Oseberg, where it adorned the grave of
a Viking lady who died in or around the ninth century, perhaps
ferocious Freydis, whom we will soon meet.

Knarrs measured some twenty meters by five and carried some
thirty men plus cattle and a dinghy, while warships measured up
to thirty meters overall but had a beam of not much more than

Viking knarr

JAVIER OBREGÓN

four meters. Both were usually built of oak planks caulked with tar and seal blubber, and their long oars pierced their gunwales. Their woolen square sail was supported by a rope net, and their mast was held up by leather stays. They steered with a "steer board," a large paddle attached to the right-hand side of the stern; hence the word *starboard.* They could not sail close to the wind, but the Vikings developed a technique of sailing and rowing at the same time that enabled them to navigate in straits and rivers.

Searching for pasture and for timber, the Norsemen in their knarrs became daring blue-water sailors. They had no magnetic compass, but to "run down the latitudes" by day they used a rudimentary gnomon, which consisted of a small vertical staff in the center of a wooden disk marked with concentric circles. When held vertically up to the sun, the extent of the staff's shadow within the circles indicated the sun's declination, which, at any given time of the year, is constant so long as the observer follows a given latitude. This was essential in the north, where the polestar stands so high that changes in its altitude are difficult to measure.

In their day the Norse were without known rivals as long-range navigators, for the Polynesians still hid behind their South Seas. Before the end of the ninth century, they had established themselves in Scotland, England, and Ireland. They even besieged Paris with several hundred ships and thousands of men, and the French king had to buy them off by ceding Normandy, where the Norsemen settled, whence its name. In Iceland they founded an aristocratic republic ruled by the Althing, an assembly of forty pagan priests, or *godar*.

At the end of the tenth century, Erik the Red, fleeing Icelandic justice beause of a crime committed by his slaves, sailed to Greenland with a fleet of twenty-five knarrs and founded a colony, which eventually grew to some three thousand souls. The Icelandic sagas, a body of oral history usually recited at feasts by sagamen, or *thulirs,* were similar to the bardic poems that culminated in Homer (the word *saga* has the same root as *sagen* in German, "to say" in English). The sagas were not written down until the thirteenth century (the originals are in the Royal Library at Copenhagen), and they were not communicated to the rest of the world until they were published in Latin in the eighteenth century. Consequently, though the sagas tell us how the Norsemen sailed west from Greenland in the eleventh century, the world at large did not hear of the Norse explorations of Newfoundland until seven centuries after they occurred. Nevertheless, having

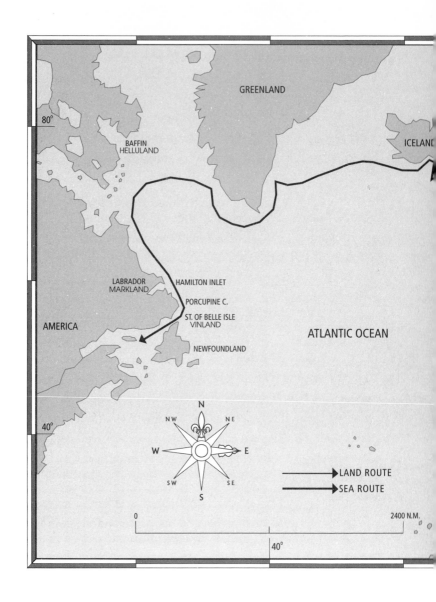

The Vikings

retraced the Norsemen's route to the West, I am convinced that they did indeed follow the coast of Baffin Island to Labrador and Newfoundland. It is worth summarizing what the sagas tell us (including some humorous details not usually included in history books) and reviewing the reasons that lead us to believe that the Norsemen in fact reached America.

Toward the end of the tenth century, Biarni Herjolfsson set sail from Iceland for Greenland, drifted off his latitude, and came to a heavily wooded coast. With a north wind, he followed the coast south, keeping it to starboard (his right) in the mist. When the fog cleared, he was able to steer by the sun past a land of glaciers and dark, flat rocks. The wind veered to the southwest and Biarni returned to Greenland, where he sold his knarr to Leif Eriksson, son of Erik the Red, whom the sagas describe as "Leif the fortunate," tall, strong, imposing, and prudent.

Up to this time the Norsemen had been pagans, and the religious sagas, or Eddas, give us a rough picture of their pantheon, which was not unlike that of the Greeks and the Polynesians. Thor was king of the Aesir, the principal gods, and, like Zeus, hurled lightning and thunder against the giants; Odin, the magician, was like Orpheus; mischievous Loki was like Eros; Frey was the god of crops; and his sister Freya was, like Aphrodite, goddess of love. But around the year 1000 the Althing decreed that Christianity would be the religion of Iceland, and Leif became the first Christian in the Greenland colony.

Fifteen years after Biarni's return, Leif decided to seek the woods and pasture that Greenland lacked in the land Biarni had sighted, and in the first summer of the eleventh century he set sail

Helluland

Markland

westward with thirty-five men. Erik, his father, had refused to convert to Christianity, and his wife had left him; so he resolved to go west with Leif. But when his horse threw him, he changed his mind and decided to stay home. The sagas do not tell whether he considered the fall an omen or if his bones creaked so much that he was glad to jump ship.

The sagas describe the coasts Leif explored in the west with a northeast wind: first Helluland, with its glaciers and dark, flat rocks; then Markland, where spruce trees stood over the Furdurstrandir, long white beaches across which streams flowed into the sea; and finally Vinland, beyond a strait in the mouth of which Leif passed an island surrounded by currents. From there Leif reached a cape that pointed north, and here he ran aground. When the tide lifted his ship, he sailed into the mouth of a river and anchored in a lake, where he built shelters. There was pasture all winter, and wild wheat; the lake never froze over, there were plenty of salmon, and the night was never three times as

long as the day, as it was in Iceland and Greenland. So Leif stayed
the rest of the summer and one winter. All this I followed with
Admiral Sam Morison and Jim Nields, and I can vouch that the
saga's descriptions are accurate.

Archaeologists recovering Vinland

In Vinland grapes (or berries) were plentiful, and Tyrker,
Leif's German godfather, made wine and got drunk, giving Vinland its name. It has been argued whether it is possible to make
wine so far north, but berries may have fermented by themselves
in Vinland's summer, as *marula* does in Africa (I have seen apes

totter away from a feast of fermented *marula*). Linguists have another explanation for the name: *Vinland* can mean "grassland."

Perhaps climatic changes give us the best answer. By sampling the polar ice caps and analyzing tree rings, climatologists have deduced that from the fifth to the eleventh centuries it was so cold in southern Europe that the Tiber and the Nile froze over, and so warm in the north that wine was produced in England, and perhaps in Newfoundland. Greenland, therefore, may well have been greener than it is now; but the sagas say that Erik called it green to attract settlers. After the twelfth century, the climate fluctuated wildly and the seas were hazardous; then the north passed through a minor glacial period, which ended the age of the Vikings. In any case, the Norsemen's exploration of lands to the west, which was to end in a massacre, began on a festive note, and in the spring Leif returned to Greenland with a fair wind, a good cargo of wood, and perhaps some wine.

Two years later, Thorvald, another of Erik's sons, went back to Vinland with thirty men to spend two winters in the shelters Leif refused to give him but agreed to let him use. Thorvald's men explored a coast to the west of Vinland, along which there were many islands, then sailed east and north, where they ran aground, breaking their keel on a promontory that they called Cape Keel. This time the Norsemen were welcomed by Skrellings, dark barbarians who attacked from the sea in leather canoes and planted an arrow under Thorvald's arm. He was buried on the Cape of the Crosses, and in the spring, the surviving Norsemen hurried back to Greenland. Some three years later Thorfinn Karlsefni mounted an expedition of three knarrs and two hundred men and women. Freydis, Leif's domineering half sister, also joined the expedition with her husband, another Thorvald, who, according to the sagas, was a weakling who had married her for her money. Thorfinn also took along his wife, Gudrid, the widowed daughter-in-law of Erik, a beautiful woman, who, though a Christian, could still sing the *vardlok*, the old witch-songs.

The sagas, with what seems to me to be a Nordically wry sense of humor, tell us an extraordinary story about her. When Thorstein Eriksson, Gudrid's first husband, died in an epidemic that caught the couple while they were guests in Greenland, Gudrid sat on her host's lap and was consoled in his arms. Suddenly Thorstein's cadaver arose and prophesied her future: she would remarry and be widowed in Iceland; then she would go in pilgrimage to Rome; and upon her return to Iceland, she would take a nun's vows and build a church. According to the sagas, all of this eventually came to pass, and three of Gudrid's descendants eventually became bishops. We presume she never again had to sit on anyone's lap.

Just as Leif had done, Karlsefni crossed a strait with an island at its entrance, landed in Vinland, and managed to stay for three winters, during which time it snowed only once. Exploring to the south, they reached Hop, "the Bay of Tides," where they dug trenches in the beach to strand halibut. It has been proposed that this was the Bay of Fundy, where tides sometimes reach fourteen meters, but there is no evidence to show that the Vikings ever sailed that far south. In this expedition it was the women who distinguished themselves: Gudrid gave birth to Snorri, the first

European born in America, and Freydis stripped to the waist and advanced on the Skrellings, pounding her chest with a short sword as if on a drum. Naturally, the Skrellings retired in disorder. Nevertheless, they kept coming out of the woods to trade skins for milk, but they soon turned nasty, so Karlsefni set a bull on them. In the end, the expeditionaries decided to return to Greenland.

Finally, around the year 1014, the indomitable Freydis convinced the brothers Helgi and Finnbogi to sail to Vinland with two knarrs to cut timber. Once there, Freydis had an idea: she threw the brothers out of Leif's shelters and convinced her husband that they had tried to seduce her, which made him so jealous that he and his men massacred the brothers while Freydis took care of the women. In spring, sole owners of all the timber they had cut, they returned to Greenland, and once there, Freydis threatened to kill anyone who told the story. Nevertheless Leif, her half brother, suspected the worst. He tortured three of her men until they told the truth, and he prophesied that her descendants would never prosper, which they didn't.

On the northernmost tip of Newfoundland, in front of the island and strait of Belle Isle, Anse-aux-Meadows lies in the shallow Bay of Épaves. The grassy shore is dotted with blackberry bushes and watered by a stream that runs down from a lake. Here Norwegian archaeologist Helge Ingstad found the remains of shelters like those found in Greenland, a few implements, and charcoal that has been carbon-dated to the eleventh century, all of which leaves little doubt that this is Vinland. If one crosses the strait and sails northwest along Labrador's black and forbidding

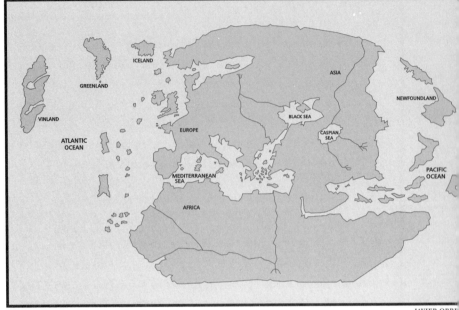

Vinland map in New Foundland

JAVIER OBRE

coast, which is visited by icebergs even in summer, one rounds
Cape Porcupine near Hamilton Inlet. There, fifty kilometers of
white beaches stretch out in the shade of a beautiful stand of
spruce, and several streams flow into the sea; surely this is the
Furdurstrandir of Markland. Finally, further north and less than
five degrees from the Artic Circle, the dark and rocky coast of
Baffin Island seems perfect for Helluland.

The Norsemen certainly hit upon America, but the Skrellings,
and perhaps our climatologists' "hazardous seas," caused them
to forget it, while the sagas remained unknown to Western civilization. Vinland vanished until the eighteenth century, and

Hop perhaps forever, though nineteenth-century archaeologists searched for it from Labrador to New York. Supposedly runic stones have been found as far west as Minnesota, but the runic alphabet disappeared before the Vikings could have gone that far. The mother colony on Greenland also disappeared, and the skeletons that have been found there are of small, undernourished people, surely victims of the Little Ice Age (1430–1850), which closed their ports.

Not long ago, Yale bought a map that purports to show Vinland. Samuel Eliot Morison immediately declared it false because of the colors of its ink. I also doubted, because in front of Asia it shows an unmistakable but inverted image of Newfoundland, and it seems clear to me that whoever added it forgot that islands do not "turn tail" when one flattens the sphere. The Vinland Map has since been declared false.

Other Vikings, the Swedish Varangians or *Russ,* opened up Russia by carrying their ships from the Baltic Sea into the Volga River and down the Don, or up

Idrisi's map of the globe

SPAIN

MEDITERRANEAN SEA

R. NIGER

R. NILE

ARABIA

ASIA (INDIA)

AFRICA AND TERRA INCOGNITA

JAVIER OBREGÓN

the Occidental Dvina and down the Dnieper to the Black Sea and to Constantinople. In southwest Russia and in Sicily they met the Muslims and could have informed them that their countrymen had found land beyond the Atlantic, but apparently they did not, for Mohammed Idrisi, who made a Mapamundi for Norse king Roger II of Sicily, showed only one landmass, Eurasia, bounded east and west by the Infinite Ocean.

Epilogue

The Greeks broadened their world to the ends of the Mediterranean and of the Black Sea, and the Polynesians across the Indian Ocean and the Pacific. Theirs were the stars, the winds, the claw sail, the astrolabe, and the first estimation of the circumference of the globe. Between them, they explored more than half of that circumference, yet they never met.

The Muslims traversed Eurasia from the shores of the Atlantic to the Isles of Spice, which look out onto the Pacific, and the Vikings crossed the North Atlantic to Newfoundland. Theirs were the dhow, which became a caravel, the gnomon, and the rudder. Yet they never ventured out into either ocean.

In the twelfth century, Mohammed Idrisi, a Muslim cartographer whose ancestors had reached the Pacific from the west,

Astrolabe

drew a *mappae mundi* for Roger II Guiscard, a descendant of the Vikings whose ancestors had reached Newfoundland; yet Idrisi's globe still showed a single landmass bathed by a single ocean.

Nevertheless, without these people, the Renaissance might not have achieved what it required: a world encompassed. And who knows: the Russians and the Americans might not so soon have taken the first steps into space.

So the Greeks, Polynesians, Muslims, and Vikings were the forerunners.

Select Bibliography

Apollonius of Rhodes. *The Argonautica.* Trans. R. C. Seaton. Loeb
Classics. Cambridge: Harvard University Press, 1967.

Calder, Michael. *The Weather Machine.* New York: Viking, 1975.

Grimal, Pierre. *Dictionnaire de la Mythologie Grecque et Romaine.*
Paris: Presses Universitaires de France, 1958.

Haugen, Einar. *Voyages to Vinland: The First American Saga.* New
York: A. A. Knopf, 1942.

Homer. *The Odyssey.* Trans. E. V. Rieu. Baltimore: Penguin Books, 1969.

Khaldún, Ibn, *Magaddima.* Trans. F. Rosenthal. New York: Hakluyt
Society, 1958.

Morison, J. S. and Williams, R. T. *Greek Oared Ships, 900–322 B.C.*
Cambridge: Harvard University Press, 1968.

Needham, Joseph. *Science and Civilisation in China.* Cambridge,
Eng.: Cambridge University Press, 1954.

Olsen, Olaf and Ole Crumlin-Pedersen. *The Skuldelev Ships.* Rpt. from
ACTA ARCHAELOGICA XXXVIII. Copenhagen, 1967.

Index

stars *(cont'd)*
    navigation, 23, 34–37, 42. *See also*
        specific star
    sterns: of ships, 29, 31, 32–33
    sun, 11–12, 13, 15, 18, 22, 82, 85,
        100, 108–9, 112. *See also* Helios

Tahiti, 12
Tamerland, 95
Tangiers, 83
Tarara. *See* Shaula
Tau Mailap (Altair), 35
Tawhiri, 9, 11
Teiresias, 83, 90
Telemachus, 32, 88, 89, 90
Telepylos, 80, 82
temperate zones, 15, 20, 35, 37
threnoi (Greek beams), 30
thunder, 18, 112
Thynias, island of, 55
tides, 22
Timur, 10, 33
Tiphys, 44, 52, 53, 55
Titans, 8, 9, 48
Tokelau wind, 20
tonga winds, 20
tonos (Greek stays), 30, 45
trade winds, 18, 35, 40, 106
tramontana winds, 20, 76–77
Trinacria, island of, 85
tropics, 15, 18, 20, 35–37

Troy, 25, 29, 48, 50, 68, 71, 74, 83
Tunis, strait of, 71
Tyrrhenian Sea, 80

Uranus, 6, 8

Varangians, 119–20
Vega, 28, 35
Vikings, 107, 115, 116–17, 119–20,
    121, 123. *See also* Norsemen
Vinland, 113, 114–19

warships, Viking, 107–8
winds: and Argonauts, 48, 49, 50–51,
    52, 53, 55, 57, 58, 60, 63, 66; and
    climate, 18; and clouds, 18–19; and
    currents, 20, 22; and directions, 20;
    and latitude, 18–20, 28; and legacy
    of Greeks and Polynesians, 121; and
    Muslims, 95; and Norsemen, 112,
    113, 115; and Odysseus, 82, 83,
    85–86, 87; and Polynesians, 10, 20,
    40; and sails, 30, 33; and ships, 31;
    and tides, 22; types of, 20. *See also*
    type of wind

Yale University, 119

zephyr winds, 20, 52, 57, 58, 78–79,
    86
Zeus, 8, 12, 13, 18, 54, 61, 84, 86
Zeus' Cape, 58